Kwakiutl Village on Salmon River, Vancouver Island.

INDIANS OF
THE NORTHWEST COAST

By PLINY EARLE GODDARD

NEW YORK
COOPER SQUARE PUBLISHERS, INC.
1972

Originally Published, 1934
Reprinted 1972 by Cooper Square Publishers, Inc.
59 Fourth Avenue, New York, N. Y. 10003
International Standard Book No. 0-8154-0428-X
Library of Congress Catalog Card No. 72-81191

Printed in the United States of America

The Northwest Coast Hall

As used in this book, Northwest Coast means the North Pacific Coast of North America, or the territory along the coast extending from the Columbia River in the State of Washington to Mount St. Elias in southern Alaska. Part of this territory lies in Washington, part in British Columbia, and the remainder in southern Alaska. The Indian tribes of this region have certain characteristics in common, so it is customary to treat them as a group, or a culture area. This area is often called the North Pacific Coast Culture Area, but as a matter of convenience the author refers to it as the Northwest Coast, and so the museum hall in which the exhibit for the tribes of this area are arranged, is frequently called the Northwest Coast Hall and also the North Pacific Coast Hall. Since Morris K. Jesup, a former President of the Museum, contributed largely to the development of this hall, it is officially known as the Jesup North Pacific Hall.

As you enter this hall, on the west side are the exhibits for the Nootka, Kwakiutl, and Tlingit; on the east side, for the Interior Salish people, the Thompson and Lillooet, the Coast Salish, Bella Coola, Tsimshian, and Haida. In the central aisle is a large dug-out Haida canoe containing life-sized figures representing a visiting Chilkat chief and his followers and, in addition, miniature models of a Kwakiutl village and a family group illustrating their industries.

On the walls and columns of this hall are many typical examples of the wood carving of the area, including masks, grave monuments, house posts, and totem poles. A series of murals by Will S. Taylor illustrates, on the west wall, daily life and industries of the several tribes, and on the east, ceremonial and religious performances.   The painting on the south wall depicts games and other peaceful occupations while the companion picture on the opposite wall represents a returning war party celebrating a victory.

The collections here shown were secured through Museum expeditions and through purchase.   Two very complete and extensive collections, mainly from the Tlingit, made by Lieutenant George T. Emmons during many years spent among these people, were purchased in 1888 and 1894.   Heber R. Bishop in 1882 presented a collection, mostly from the Haida, and gathered in part by Doctor J. W. Powell.   With few exceptions, the remainder of the collections for the area were secured through the work of the Jesup North Pacific Expedition, planned and organized by Professor F. W. Putnam and Professor Franz Boas, supervised by Professor Boas, and financed by the late Morris K. Jesup when President of the Museum.   The Nootka collection was made by Filip Jacobsen and George Hunt, the Kwakiutl and Bella Coola collections by Professor Boas and George Hunt, and the Thompson and Lillooet collections by James Teit.

PREFACE

The collections of ethnological specimens illustrating the life of the tribes of North America north of Mexico are at present arranged in four exhibition halls on the first floor of the Museum. These are: first, a hall devoted to the tribes east of the Mississippi and northern and eastern Canada; second, the peoples of the great plains between the Rocky Mountains and the Mississippi; third, the southwestern region where are found the Pueblo and the Navajo, Apache, and Pima; and fourth, the Northwest Coast. At the rear of the Northwest Coast Hall one enters an alcove in which the Eskimo collections are displayed.

The author of this book died in 1928. This second edition is issued with a minimum of revision, the text standing essentially as originally written. In 1922 the author visited these tribes, the Indian villages of the coast of British Columbia in the company of the late Doctor C. F. Newcombe and the Tlingit villages of Alaska under the guidance of Lieutenant George T. Emmons. The illustrations, and, for the most part, the data embodied in the text are taken from the publications of the Jesup North Pacific Expedition.

THE EDITOR

CONTENTS

PREFACE 5

CHAPTER I

INTRODUCTION 13

Habitat: Tribes. Topography. Climate. Trails. Flora. Fauna. Early History: Discovery. Spaniards. Captain Cook. De la Perouse. Trading Ships. Vancouver's Survey. Mackenzie. Fur Trade. Russians.

CHAPTER II

MATERIAL CULTURE 25

Houses: Salish. Nootka. Kwakiutl. Chilkat. Platforms. Canoes. Work in Wood: Tools. Felling. Splitting Planks. Bending Wood. Dugout Dishes. Canoe-making. Sewing Wood. Basketry and Textiles: Nets. Mat-making. Basketry. Tlingit Baskets. Cedarbark Blankets. Chilkat Blankets. Salish Blankets. Food Gathering: Whaling. Hunting Porpoises. Sealing. Fishing. Shellfish. Vegetable Food. Raising Tobacco. Land Animals. Dress and Decoration: Footgear. Men's Clothing. Women's Dress. Tattooing. Deformed Heads.

CHAPTER III

SOCIAL AND POLITICAL ORGANIZATION 85

Social Distinctions: Septs. Chiefs. Rivalry of Chiefs. Feasts. Inherited Duties. Exogamous Divisions. Puberty. Burial Customs: Tree Burial. Canoe Burial. Cremation. Memorial Columns. Marriage: Selection of Mates. Marriage Customs. Games. Warfare.

CHAPTER IV

RELIGION AND CEREMONIAL LIFE 110

Religious Beliefs: Supreme Being. Haida Deities. Bella Coola Deities. Gods of the Kwakiutl. Religious Practices: Ceremonial Purity. Offerings. Taboos. Shamanism. Winter Ceremonies: Kwakiutl Ceremonies. Magical Performances. Supernatural Visitors. Haida Ceremonies. Tlingit Ceremonies. Potlatch: The Future World. Mythology and Folklore: Raven Myths. Family Traditions.

CHAPTER V

ART 139
    Textile Decoration. Carving. Grotesque Art. Totem Poles.
    Conventionalizations.   Carved Ornamentation.   Rearrange-
    ments and Dissections. Symmetry.
BIBLIOGRAPHY 163
INDEX 167

MAP AND ILLUSTRATIONS

Kwakiutl Village on Salmon River, Vancouver Island . *Frontispiece*

Ethnological Map of the Northwest Coast . . . *opposite* 13

The Valley of the Bella Coola River navigated by Mackenzie in
    1793. Photograph by H. I. Smith 18

Method of erecting House Posts. Kwakiutl 27

Skidegate Village on Queen Charlotte Islands. Haida . . 28

House with Modernized Front. Haida 28

Method of raising House Beams. Kwakiutl 29

House at Klukwan Village. Tlingit 30

Fishing Village at Kisgagas on a Tributary of the Skeena River,
    British Columbia. Photograph by C. M. Barbeau . . . 30

Interior of House showing two Terraces with Fire below and Sleep-
    ing Compartments above. House of Chief Weir at Masset, a
    Haida Village 32

The Northern Type of Canoe with Projecting Bow and Stern.
    Haida 34

Bailers for Canoes. Kwakiutl 35

Paddles 35

Long-handled Adze 36

Set of Seven Wedges in the End of a Log 37

Wedges used for Splitting Boards from Logs. Kwakiutl . . 37

Hand Hammers 38

Carving Knives and Drill with Bone Point. Kwakiutl . . 39

Chisels with Bone Blades. Kwakiutl 40

Hand Adze with Stone Blade. Nootka 41

Hunter's Boxes and Board Cut for Folding to make Such a Box.
    Kwakiutl 42

Wooden Vessels. Kwakiutl 42

Oil Dishes dug out of Alder. Kwakiutl 43

The Joined Corner of Box with Stitching Indicated. Kwakiutl . 44

Box with Projection on Lid. Kwakiutl 44

Method of Joining Boards by Sewing. Kwakiutl . . . 45

Spindle used for Nettle Fiber. Kwakiutl 46

Details of Square and Diagonal Mat Weaving. Kwakiutl . . 46

Twilled Cedarbark Belts. Kwakiutl 47

Details of Tlingit Basketry 49

Bag illustrating Open-Twining 49

Spruce Root Basket, Bird-cage Stitch and Double Basket of
    Checkerwork. Kwakiutl 50

Spruce Root Hat with its Cedarbark Cover. Kwakiutl . . 50

Detail of Openwork Mat and Twilled Cedarbark Pouch.
  Kwakiutl 51
Berrying Basket with Carrying Strap and a Carrying Strap used
  by Mountain Goat Hunters. Kwakiutl 51
Tlingit Baskets 52
Implements for Shredding Cedarbark. Kwakiutl . . . 54
Beater for Cedarbark. Kwakiutl 54
Detail of suspending a Chilkat Blanket 55
Pattern Board from which Women weave Chilkat Blankets . . 56
Spindle Whorls 57
Float made of Seal Bladder. Kwakiutl 60
Harpoon for Salmon. Kwakiutl 61
Halibut Hooks set in Pairs. Kwakiutl 62
Dam and Fish Trap. Kwakiutl 64
Dam and Fish Basket for Salmon. Kwakiutl. 64
Trolling Hook for Salmon and Clubs for killing Habibut.
  Kwakiutl 65
Salmon Trap for Narrow Streams. Kwakiutl. . . . 66
Weir for Eulachon Fishing. Kwakiutl 66
Salmon Drying. Chilkat River, Alaska 68
Eulachon or Candlefish in Storage 70
Rendering Eulachon Oil in a Canoe by Means of Hot Stones . 70
Pile Drivers 71
Fish Basket. Kwakiutl 72
Crab Net. Kwakiutl 72
Herring Rake. Kwakiutl 73
Digging-sticks. Kwakiutl 74
Tongs 75
Bird Spear. Nootka 76
Bows and Arrows. Kwakiutl 76
Spring Trap used for Bear, Deer, and Smaller Animals. Kwakiutl 78
Deadfalls. Kwakiutl 78
Woman's Apron. Kwakiutl 80
Ornaments: a, Anklet; b, Bracelet. Hair Ornament of Dentalium
  Shells. Kwakiutl 80
Hat on which Whale Hunting is Depicted. Nootka . . 81
Cradle with Cedarbark Bedding. Kwakiutl . . . 82
Nose Ornaments of Abalone Shell. Kwakiutl . . . 83
Kwakiutl Woman with Deformed Head 84
A Copper: Design, Horned Owl 89
A Chief with his Broken Copper. Kwakiutl 90

Tree Burial near Alert Bay, B. C. Kwakiutl   99
Grave Post with Cavity in the Back of the Figure in which an In-
    cinerated Body has been placed. Wrangell, Tlingit   .   .   . 99
Memorial Columns, Anthony Island. Haida. Photograph by
    Doctor C. F. Newcombe   101
Double-Edged and Double-Bladed Knife, made of Bone of Whale.
    Tlingit   108
Warclub made of Whale's Rib. Tlingit   108
Jade Weapon inserted in Wooden Handle. Tlingit   .   .   . 108
Model representing a Shaman with Raven Symbols. Haida   .   . 118
Model of a Shaman's Grave Box. Haida   119
A Youth showing the Hemlock Decoration of a Novice. Kwakiutl 123
Fool Dancers of the Winter Ceremony. Kwakiutl   .   . 125
Cannibal Society of Winter Ceremony. Kwakiutl.   .   .   . 125
Checker Design on a Mat. Kwakiutl   139
Decoration produced by Varying Direction of Elements in Twilling.
    Kwakiutl   139
Baskets illustrating Geometrical Designs. Tlingit   .   .   . 140
Haida Village of Tanu, Queen Charlotte Islands. Photograph by
    Doctor C. F. Newcombe 142
Painted House Front: Thunderbird carrying off a Whale. Alert
    Bay. Kwakiutl.   142
Support of a Grave Box carved to represent a Beaver wearing a
    Hat. Haida   143
Masks representing Supernatural Beings. Bella Coola   .   . 144
Double Mask: Closed, Raven as a Bird; Open, Raven as a Man.
    Haida 145
Harpoon Rest for Bow of Canoe. Kwakiutl 145
Models of Haida Totem Poles   146
Front and Back of a Box: Moon as a Bird (above); Mountain
    Goat (below)   147
Totem Pole in the Museum. Haida   148
Memorial Column in the Museum. Haida   148
Totem Pole. Haida   149
Facial Paintings. Haida   150
Rattle with Hawk Design. Tlingit   151
Mountain Sheep Horn Dish representing a Hawk. Tlingit .   . 151
Grease Dish in Shape of a Seal. Tlingit 151
Masks and Rattle. Woman with Labret is represented in 2.
    Haida 152
Settee with Family Emblems carved on the Back. Kwakiutl   . 153
Paint Brushes. Kwakiutl 153

Club representing a Killer-whale with Dorsal Fin bent down.
    Tlingit   154
Bow of the Large Canoe in the Museum   154
Painting of Shark cut Apart and Spread Open.   Haida   .   .   155
Tattoo Designs.   Haida   155
Painting from a House Front showing a Bear as if cut Along the
    Back, giving a Symmetrical Treatment Either Side of Circular
    Door.   Tsimshian   156
Animal Representations adjusted to Hats.   Haida   .   .   .   157
Shirt with Designs Similar to Those on Blankets.   Tlingit   .   .   158
Dancing Apron.   Tlingit   158
Designs on Chilkat Blankets   159
Designs on Chilkat Blankets   160
Design on Chilkat Blanket: Positions of Anatomical Parts are
    Indicated   161

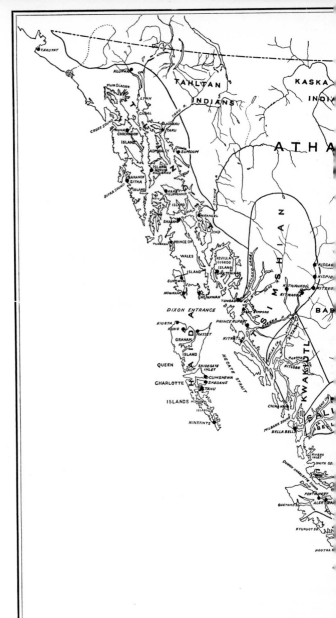

ETHNOLOGICAL MAP

OF THE

NORTHWEST COAST

AFTER NEWCOMBE

SCALE
0 10 20 30 40 50   100 MILES

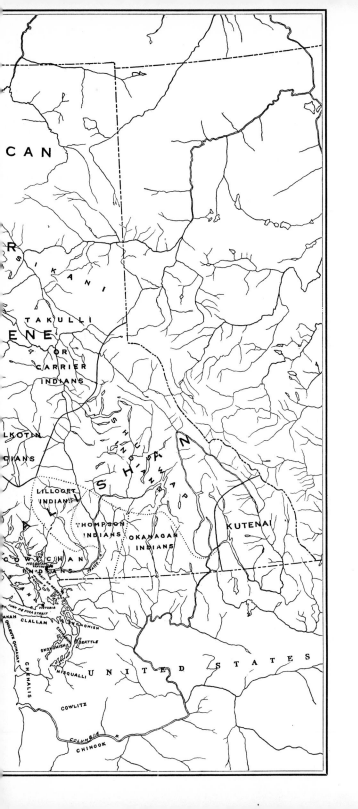

CHAPTER I
INTRODUCTION
HABITAT

The Northwest Coast is the land of the totem pole. Its aboriginal inhabitants are further distinguished by their large rectangular wooden houses and dug-out canoes, scanty dress, and their dependence upon the products of the sea for food. They also placed great value upon purity of family descent and the virtue of benevolence in the disposition of property; but most conspicuous of all their traits is their highly original grotesque art.

Tribes. Beginning in the northern part of this area, we note the Tlingit tribe, one of the best known divisions of which is the Chilkat. Beyond the Tlingit, along the coast, are the Eskimo who, though resembling somewhat in culture the peoples of the Northwest Coast, are much more closely affiliated, physically, linguistically, and culturally, with the main body of Eskimo. In the interior toward the east the neighbors of the Tlingit, are Athapascan-speaking people. While they have been somewhat influenced by their coast neighbors they may be unhesitatingly classified with their relatives further to the east and in the valley of the Yukon. South of the Tlingit are the Haida, who in many respects may be regarded as typically of the Northwest Coast culture. Though geographically near the extreme northern boundaries of the area, culturally they represent the focal point of Northwest Coast culture. Their neighbors on the east are the Tsimshian-speaking tribes of closely similar culture, living mainly on the Nass and Skeena rivers, their villages extending for quite a distance up these rivers into a somewhat different environment and a less humid climate; they maintained, however, a life quite similar

13

to that of the coast people, securing through trade those products which are naturally limited to the sea. East of the Tsimshian are Athapascan tribes, strikingly different from them in nearly every respect.

As we proceed southward, the tribes become different both in appearance and in mode of life. It will be more convenient to discuss them by referring first to their language. They belong to two separate linguistic stocks: the Wakashan and the Salish. The former consists of two dialectic groups, the Kwakiutl and Nootka; the main body of the Kwakiutl live on the northern part of Vancouver Island, the neighboring smaller islands, and the adjacent mainland to the east. Geographically isolated to the north are two Kwakiutl dialects: the Haisla and the Heiltsuk, the best known tribes belonging to these groups being the Bella Bella, living on Fitzhugh Sound and the Kitlope on Gardiner Channel. They are separated from the other Kwakiutl and closely affiliated with a Salish-speaking people, the Bella Coola, who live on Burke Channel and its extensions. The Nootka are confined to the west coast of Vancouver Island, unless one includes with them the Makah, a tribe closely related in speech, living on the American side of the Straits of Juan de Fuca.

The main body of the Salish, from whom the Bella Coola have become separated, occupy a large and continuous area in southern British Columbia and the western portion of the State of Washington. They occupy the eastern part of Vancouver Island, south of Cape Mudge, and the southern end of the Island around Victoria. There can be no doubt that the Salish people on Vancouver Island should be included with those having the typical Northwest Coast culture. It is on the mainland of British Columbia and the State of Washington that the boundaries are less definite.

Salish-speaking peoples live along the Fraser River and occupy its large tributary, the Thompson River. These interior Salish tribes, the Thompson, Lillooet, and Shuswap, have never been considered as possessing the culture of the coast peoples since their houses, dress, food, religion, and art, are quite different not only from those of the Northwest Coast, but from their other neighbors as well.

In respect to such traits as rectangular houses, canoes, dress, food in part, and the regard for birth and wealth, there is an extension of the northwest culture southward down the coast of Washington and Oregon and into California, as far as Humboldt Bay. To place a definite line between this southern extension of attenuated culture into California and the Straits of Juan de Fuca, where it existed rather typically, would be quite arbitrary.

The difficulty is, however, more a logical than a practical one. For the present purpose, it will be sufficient to treat as a unit the culture participated in by the tribes enumerated above; those of Tlingit speech,. the Haida, the Tsimshian, the Bella Bella, Bella Coola, Kwakiutl, Nootka, and the Salish on Vancouver Island and about the delta of the Fraser.

Topography. In many respects the northern Pacific coast of America resembles that of Scandinavia. Both regions have been subject to remarkable depression, so that the valleys are flooded by the sea and the mountains rise abruptly from the water. Long arms of the ocean cut deeply into the land and the streams flowing into them are usually rushing mountain torrents. The heavy precipitation results in the steep mountains being covered with forests or snow.

Along the coast are several very large islands and innumerable smaller ones, separated from each other and from the mainland by navigable straits. At the southern boundary of the area is Vancouver Island, three hundred miles long and from forty to eighty miles wide. At the north it is separated from the Queen Charlotte Islands by Queen Charlotte Sound which is about forty miles wide. The two larger of the last-named islands are Moresby at the south and Graham which lies north of it. Together they are about one hundred eighty miles long, the greatest width of Graham Island is about sixty miles. North of the Queen Charlotte Islands is Dixon Entrance, cutting them off from the islands of Alaska, Prince of Wales, Baranof, Chichagof, and other islands. Between these large outlying islands and the mainland are many others of varying sizes.

It will be readily seen then that on such a coast because of the large number of inlets and the innumerable islands the shore line is very long. This is in very great contrast with the coast of California, where the islands are few, and the coast so abrupt that the tide flows but a short distance up the rivers. On the whole, the northwest coast of America is an exceedingly favorable region for the development of a culture almost entirely dependent upon canoes for travel and transportation and upon the sea for its food supply. The sheltered channels are so continuous that the larger dug-out canoes can be brought quite safely from Skagway, at the mouth of the Chilkat River, to the southern end of Puget Sound, provided the weather is favorable for crossing the two or three more exposed stretches of water.

Climate. The climate, though somewhat resembling that of the west coast of Europe, divides more sharply into a rainy and a dry season. In the south the rainy season occupies the months between October and April; in the north, it is longer and the rains heavier.

The warm Japan current follows the curve of the coast from Alaska southward, moderating the climate and preventing the snow from remaining any length of time in the low altitudes over the entire area. Influenced as it is by the mountain ranges which cause the precipitation, the rainfall varies greatly according to the particular locality. Fogs and mists are more common nearer the ocean, while the heavier rains usually occur on the ocean side of the higher mountain ranges. The climate grows progressively more severe as one leaves the outer fringe of islands and proceeds toward the Cascade Range, so that the river valleys of the mainland have rather severe winters and hot summers.

Trails. For the most part, the interior of the larger islands and the mainland was untraversed by the natives. The greater part of the area is covered by steep and rugged mountains difficult of ascent. The entire area is so heavily forested that travel on foot is extremely difficult. Moreover, because of the broken nature of the seacoast, the waterways formed the natural highways of travel so that, with the exception of a few trails which crossed to the interior, there was little travel by land. Nearly everywhere the native settlements were on the ocean shore or along the navigable rivers. Vancouver Island was crossed by trails at several places, one was from the head of Alberni Sound to the east coast, another was from Nimkish Lake to Kyukuot and Nootka sounds, and a third led from Fort Rupert to Quatsino Sound.

Farther north were the so-called "grease trails" used by trading parties, particularly in bartering for eulachon oil.

Flora. The whole region, from California northward, was heavily forested, with hemlock, Douglas fir, spruce, and cedar; yellow cedar was more prevalent

The Valley of the Bella Coola River navigated by Mackenzie in 1793.   Photograph by H. I. Smith

18

in the north and red cedar in the south. Along rocky points where it is difficult for large trees to maintain themselves, madroñas or arbutus and a few oaks are found. In the river bottoms are large areas where alder and cottonwood predominate. Everywhere in the forest there is a heavy undergrowth of blueberry and huckleberry bushes, of vine maple, thimbleberries, and salmon berries. This density of vegetation is directly related to the heavy rainfall. Ferns tend to take the place of grasses which are practically unknown, except in the swamps, but a heavy growth of moss forms a thick carpet underfoot and covers the branches of trees.

Fauna. The fauna of the area varies considerably. Of land mammals the most important were deer, elk, mountain goat, and along the courses of the northern rivers, moose. Bear were also plentiful throughout the entire region, although the grizzly and brown bear were common only in the north. Sea mammals were of much greater importance to the economic life than land mammals; the chief of these were the whale, seal, sea-lion, and porpoise. The sea-otter was an important source of clothing and in later years, a source of trade wealth.

Above all, however, the natives of the Northwest Coast depended for their chief food supply on fish, especially the salmon which was the great staple in the whole region, as important as was the buffalo in the Plains Area. Each spring the salmon ascended the rivers to spawn and at this time the year's supply was obtained. A variety of salt water fish, such as cod, halibut, herring, eulachon, and smelt, were important additions to the fish diet. Especially in the south, shellfish such as clams, oysters, mussels, and crabs were of considerable importance.

EARLY HISTORY

Discovery. The Pacific Coast of North America was visited first in 1578 by Francis Drake whose farthest north was at Bodega Bay, California (Lat. 38° 18′), far south of the region of our particular interest. Juan de Fuca, however, in 1592 discovered the entrance to the straits which bear his name.

The first landing on the northern coast appears to have been made in July, 1741, by the Russian explorer, Behring, and by Tschirikow, captain of one of Behring's ships. The latter anchored near Sitka and sent an officer with ten men ashore for water. The boat landed behind a point and the pre-arranged signals for safe landing were seen. When, after some days, the party failed to return, a small boat with four men was sent to learn the cause of the delay. Neither boat returned, but some days later, two boats were seen in the distance. Tschirikow, thinking his two lost boats were returning, mustered the crew on deck. But these boats were in reality manned by natives who, observing the numerous crew aboard the ship retreated hastily. The captain had no other small boats and the coast was too rough and the wind too strong to permit the ship to approach nearer to the land. He was obliged to sail away and leave his boat crews to their fate. A few days later Behring himself was in a gulf north of Cape St. Elias. He sent two boats to explore and to obtain fresh water. The crews found a deserted summer house, dried salmon, and a firedrill.

Spaniards. The first recorded voyage by the Spaniards was in 1774 when Juan Perez, in the *Santiago*, sailed from San Blas as far as the northern point of the Queen Charlotte Islands. On his return he anchored in a harbor later named Nootka Sound. The next year the Spaniards, who were establishing themselves along the southern California coast, sent three small vessels under the command of Don Juan de Ayala to explore the coast northward. Don Francisco Antonio Maurella, whose name appears in connection with several such voyages, was pilot of one of these ships and chronicler of the expedition. They stopped at Trinidad Bay, California, and then followed the coast to the neighborhood of Sitka, where they paused to explore and take on wood and water. Returning, because of scurvy, they put in at a place they named Port Bucarelli (Lat. 57° 17'), on the coast of Prince of Wales Island. A second expedition led by Don de la Bodega, with Maurella second in command, spent May and June of 1779 in the same locality, in trade with the natives.

Captain Cook. In 1778, Captain James Cook, on his third and last voyage, spent the greater part of April in Nootka Sound, where he secured a new mast and overhauled his ships, *Resolution* and *Discovery*. Although among the Nootka Cook found metals, including two silver spoons obtained from the Spaniards in 1774, it was his opinion that they had never before seen Europeans. The narrative of his voyage describes the houses, dress, and customs of the Nootka in considerable detail.

De la Perouse. Stimulated by Captain Cook's exploits under the English flag, France equipped two ships, the *Boussole* and *Astrolabe*, and sent them to explore under the leadership of J. T. O. de la Perouse. Leaving France in August, 1785, the expedition reached Cooks Inlet in June, 1786, having come by way of Cape Horn, the coast of Chile, and Easter Island. The ships were taken into a bay which de la Perouse named Port des Francais (Lat. 58° 37'), where they remained several days. The Indians, who had summer fishing villages on the shores of the bay, were constantly in contact with the ship and the camp established on an island. After losing two boat crews in the breakers at the entrance of the harbor, de la Perouse sailed down the coast, most of the time in thick weather, until he reached Monterey Bay, California.

Trading Ships. In 1786, English and American ships began visiting the Northwest Coast to secure furs, particularly sea-otter skins which they sold to the Chinese. Two ships from Bengal, belonging to the East India Company, under Captains Lorie and Guise, reached Nootka on the twenty-seventh of June of that year. Captain Hanna arrived in August of the same year. The South Sea Company, organized in England to carry on the fur trade in the North Pacific, sent out two ships, the *King George*, in command of Captain Portlock and the *Queen Charlotte* commanded by George Dixon. The ships left England in August, 1785, and spent three years in exploration and trade. Under George Dixon's name, a journal of the voyage was published giving numerous interesting details concerning the Indians of the coast, many of whom had never before seen either white men or their ships. This is the first descriptive account of the Haida and Tlingit.

Exploring the coast and trading, Captain John Meares spent the summer of 1788 cruising from Nootka Sound southward as far as Shoalwater Bay, Washington. During the summer under his direction, a schooner was built and launched at Nootka Sound and a trading post established. The next year this settlement, as well as one of Meares' ships on a return trip, was seized by a Spanish naval force which was ordered to hold the Pacific Coast against the English.

Vancouver's Survey. Soon after, a systematic survey and charting of the coast was carried out for the English government by Captain George Vancouver. Much of the surveying was done in small boats which were taken up many of the long inlets in order to distinguish the mainland from the islands. Many incidental descriptions of the natives and their customs, occur in this work as well as the first mention of the Bella Bella, perhaps also of the Bella Coola, and the Tsimshian. The Tlingit of the interior waters were often encountered by Vancouver's surveying parties. Vancouver negotiated unsuccessfully for the transfer to England of the Nootka settlement seized by the Spaniards in 1789. He left England in 1791 and returned in 1795 having spent the summers of 1792, 1793, and 1794, on the North Pacific Coast and the winters in the Hawaiian Islands.

Mackenzie. In the summer of 1793, Alexander Mackenzie traversed the continent of North America; having followed up the Peace River and its southern tributary he crossed over to the headwaters of the Fraser and journeyed down the Fraser to Blackwater River, and by trail across the Cascade Range, and down the Bella Coola to Deans Channel. He continued his journey down Burke Channel until he met natives who had seen Vancouver. In the account of this journey are descriptions of the Bella Coola villages and their fishing operations.

Fur Trade. It is not necessary to detail the history of the fur-trading companies on the coast, since the subject has been fully treated in easily accessible books. Their influence on native life was, however, very great. Astoria, established near the mouth of the Columbia in 1811 by a company organized by John Jacob Astor, was turned over to the English Northwest Company in 1813. For many years this and the Hudson Bay Company, after their consolidation, traded from Fort Vancouver, ninety miles above the mouth of the Columbia. In 1848, the territory having passed into the control of the United States, the capital of the fur trade was transferred to Victoria on Vancouver Island.

Russians. The Alaskan coast was first visited by the Russians, as is mentioned above, in 1741. A settlement was made at Sitka in 1799 by Baranoff who built a fort and brought a large number of Aleut to engage in sea-otter hunting. The Tlingit destroyed this fort in 1802 and a new one was built three miles south of it in 1804. Sitka was visited that year and the next by Urey Lisiansky whose narrative is of considerable interest. The Russians continued the settlement at Sitka until the transfer of Alaska to the United States in 1867.

CHAPTER II
MATERIAL CULTURE

Information concerning the food, clothing, housing, and industrial arts of primitive peoples is grouped under the heading of material culture. For the Indians of the Northwest Coast, their material culture may be characterized by large dependence upon sea food; extensive use of cedar, the wood for houses, canoes, utensils, etc., the bark for mats and woven costumes; and the absence of pottery and agriculture. It is not far wrong to say that these Indians used cedar for everything possible. Their skill in building houses, hollowing out canoes from large tree trunks, bending and joining wood to make boxes and other containers, commands our admiration. Large planks were split from cedar logs, the surfaces of which were dressed smooth with hand adzes. The totem poles, house posts, canoes, and other wooden objects in the Museum collections fully illustrate the expertness of these Indian workmen.

HOUSES

Salish. The houses of the southern group of tribes, including the Salish of the Fraser River Delta and the Nootka of the west coast of Vancouver Island, were long and rectangular in groundplan with a roof sloping downward to the rear walls which are lower than the front walls. Those of the Kwakiutl and of the northern tribes were more nearly square, varying considerably in size from twenty by thirty feet up to fifty by sixty. A feature common to the houses of all the tribes of the area is an independent inner main framework and an outside covering or shell. The framework persisted from year to year, even from generation to generation, while the planks of the outer shell might have been re-

moved and transported to other localities annually or
might be pulled down and afterward replaced at the death
of the house owner.   The framework of the southern
houses consisted of a double row of posts two or three feet
wide and from five to eight inches thick.   These posts
were paired along either side; separated according to the
desired width of the house.   Those forming the rear of
the house were of a lesser height than the posts at the
front.   Atop these posts were placed long beams which
served to support the roof boards, providing a very gentle
slope for the roof.   Such a house is mentioned by
George Gibbs, who states that the framework was still
standing at Fort Madison, Seattle, in 1855.   This house
had a total length of five hundred and twenty feet, a
width of sixty feet, with seventy-four posts and thirty-
seven crossbeams.   Such houses were enclosed with split
planks, placed horizontally between pairs of vertical
poles, lashed together with withes to hold them in place.
The slightly sloping roof was made by overlapping
planks which ran lengthwise of the house.   These southern houses were built with the higher long side facing
the beach.   The entrance or entrances were ordinarily
on the seaward side with an exit also in the rear.

A house of this sort was occupied by a large number of
families, each with its separate fire.   Ordinarily, each
family was assigned the space between two pairs of the
separating puncheons.   Raised platforms ran along
inside the house against the walls which were hung with
mats.   The various sections of the house were also
separated during the winter season by suspended mats.
Household property was stored on and under the side
platforms where sleeping places were also provided.
The household fires, instead of being in the center of
each section, were built in one corner of it, toward the
front where the roof was highest.   For potlatch occa-

sions a high platform was provided outside at one end of the house from which property was distributed.

Nootka. Nootka houses of this same general style were described by the earlier writers. As among the Salish, the pattern of the framework and the placing of the planks varied somewhat from one group to another. These houses, although large and entailing great labor in building, seem not to be so architecturally impressive as the houses of the north.

Method of erecting House Posts. Kwakiutl.

Kwakiutl. The ground-plan of a Kwakiutl house was laid out with a cedar rope, a line was first run from the middle of the front to the middle of the back. By doubling the rope, the distance from these middle points to the corners was easily measured. A rectangle was then secured by making the distances equal from each corner to the middle of the opposite side. The typical Kwakiutl house-frame consisted first, of two large posts fifteen to twenty feet long and two feet in diameter. These were set up six feet apart and about three feet back of what was to be the front line of the house. They were brought into an upright position by making the hole that was to receive them vertical at the front and by reënforcing it with a stout plank. An inclined plank was provided at the rear of the excavation. The base of the post was placed in the hole and the other end raised by means of levers, a round leg following down the incline to prevent the post from falling back. Across the top of these two posts a short beam was

Skidegate Village on Queen Charlotte Islands.   Haida

House with Modernized Front.   Haida

placed in semicircular depressions provided for it. At
the rear of the house two similar posts with the same
spacing were erected, but ordinarily without the cross-
beam. Next was provided a pair of horizontal beams as
long as the full depth of the house, often fifty or sixty
feet in length and eighteen inches in diameter. They
were nicely adzed, and slightly fluted, with the adze
marks left unobliterated for their decorative effect.

One method of raising these beams was to place a
log sloping from the top of one of the uprights toward
what was to be the side of the house. One end of the

Method of raising House Beams.   Kwakiutl

large beam was slid up this slope with levers and
secured in place by a pole of proper length while the
lever was re-set for the next lifting. A guard was fastened to the top of the post to prevent the beam from
slipping over when it dropped into place. The other
end of the post was brought up in a similar manner.
Another method, perhaps not so old, but simple and
effective, was to provide a cribwork in the center over
which the long beam was balanced. When one end of
the beam was pulled down toward the ground there was
room to insert another block at the raised end. The
beam was then see-sawed and the blocking placed at
the other end. In this manner the beam was easily
raised to the required height.

House at Klukwan Village.   Tlingit

Fishing Village at Kisgagas on a Tributary of the Skeena River, British Columbia.   Photograph by C. M. Barbeau

Smaller posts at the four corners supported the plates at the eaves of the house. Rows of posts were also erected at each end and supported additional longitudinal roof beams. In earlier times the house was closed in with thick planks, split and adzed, placed horizontally along the four sides and slightly overlapping to shed the water. They were lashed in place between pairs of poles with cedar withes. Similar planks extended from the eaves to the ridge so that the cracks between the first layer were covered by a second layer. At the present time planks are ordinarily placed vertically instead of horizontally. Before they are put in position a bank of earth about three feet high is placed around the house. In the front, this bank is supported by a thick plank, the upper end of which is grooved to receive the lower end of the planks forming the end wall. Their upper ends are held in place by lashing them to the crossbeams of the end and the first rafters of the roof frame. The planks of the side walls and back are embedded in the earthen banks.

These houses stood with the gable end toward the sea and had a door of moderate height near the middle. At the rear end of the house, the more desirable location, were the sleeping quarters for the owner's family, generally enclosed by a plank wall. At the rear, on the right was often a similar enclosure for the safe-keeping of ceremonial objects. This served also as a dressing room when ceremonies were in progress. Along the sides were the sleeping places of the other inmates. Each house fire was partitioned off with mats, and had a rack above it for the storage and drying of fish.

Chilkat. The houses of the northern tribes of this area were ordinarily not so large as those of the Kwakiutl. At Klukwan, a Chilkat (Tlingit) village, were rectangular houses, with longitudinal wall planks which

Interior of House showing two Terraces with Fire below and Sleeping Compartments above.   House of Chief Weir at Masset, a Haida Village

fitted into grooves in the corner posts and in an additional post placed midway of the sides.

The houses of some of the chiefs seem to have been provided with a series of earthen banks inside, forming a terrace. Many of the northern houses have carved poles placed against the middle of the front end with the house entrance through an opening cut in them.

Platforms. These houses stand in rows far enough back from the sea for a wide roadway to run along in front of them. On the seaward side of this roadway, resting on piles, are platforms, upon which much time is spent, either in work or pleasure during the fall and spring.

CANOES

Travel on the Northwest Coast was almost entirely by water. The cedar furnished an ideal wood for the construction of canoes, trees of this species often providing logs sufficiently large to build canoes of sixty or more feet in length. The wood of the cedar is soft and easily worked, yet, it is at the same time very resistent to decay. Although canoes for from one to four persons were easy to build, it was a long and difficult task to construct the larger transport and war canoes. There was a difference in type between the canoes of the northern and southern tribes of the area: in the northern type both the bow and the stern were raised and projected over the water; in the southern type, used by the Nootka and Salish, the canoe had a vertical stern and projecting bow. The canoes with projecting bows were particularly used in still protected waters; on the rivers, smaller canoes, of much the same pattern were used. Most of the tribes also constructed rather rough undifferentiated "knockabouts."

The size varied from those not more than eight feet in length and carrying only one man to the great ocean-going canoes seventy feet long and capable of carrying fifty or sixty men. A Haida example in the Museum is sixty-four feet long and has a beam of eight feet. With such canoes the Haida visited as far south as Puget Sound, seven or eight hundred miles from their home.

These canoes were propelled with paddles having a lanceolate blade and a crutch-like handle. A somewhat longer paddle was used by the steersman in controlling the direction of the craft. Canoes were also sometimes

The Northern Type of Canoe with projecting Bow and Stern. Haida.

sailed, perhaps even before contact with Europeans. The sails were made either of very thin planks lashed to a framework or of matting. A wooden sail in the Museum about nine feet square and five-eighths of an inch thick, is made of several pieces joined by sewing with spruce root. To prevent splitting, the ends of the sail are reënforced by strips of wood with the grain running in the opposite direction. Such sails were employed particularly when two canoes were lashed together and covered with house planks. If the wind were from the stern the sail was leaned up against a pile of boxes, or possibly against a short mast and the canoes were sailed before the wind. Mats were also employed as sails with a mast and a yard. In very rough weather the Nootka, at least, were accustomed to attach seal-skin floats to the gunwales of the canoes to give greater buoyancy.

Bailers for Canoes. Kwakiutl.   Paddles. c, for steering.

WORK IN WOOD

The Northwest Coast peoples excelled in woodwork. There is no other region in the world which provides at once so abundant and so satisfactory species of trees for the manufacture of articles which in the other parts of the world are made of bark or skin. Woodwork as it developed on the Northwest Coast had some unique features, such as the steaming and bending of boards to facilitate box-making.

Tools. The woodworking tools were of polished stone, shell, antler, and bone. Curiously enough, no stone tools were made by flaking. They had no axes, but two forms of adzes. One of these had the blade attached to a piece of wood from the trunk of a tree with a section of the attached limb forming an angle, furnishing a handle about two feet long. In the other kind, the blade was attached to a rectangular piece of wood, much like the handle of a carpenter's saw. The blades were of shell, bone, or stone. Chisels had wooden handles and, before metals were common, stone or bone blades.

Long-handled Adze.

Felling. Usually, it was not necessary to cut down standing trees since storms and floods furnished a sufficient supply of logs. When such logs were not available, trees were felled or slabs were split from a standing live tree. For the splitting of planks, a scarf was cut with a stone adze or chisel at the base of the tree at the side that promised the best material. In this hole a fire was built and kept under control. Then, by building a platform, workmen were able to make cuts into the tree at a height which was determined by the length of plank desired. Here he made two cuts about eighteen inches apart. The section between these cuts was split out and then wedges were driven in splitting off a long plank of the desired thickness. It seems to have been the general practice along the Northwest Coast to explore the tree first by chiseling a hole in it to make certain it was entirely sound.

Splitting Planks. Trees already on the ground, either selected from the ocean drift or windfalls, or those that had been chopped down, were severed at the desired place by building over them a fire in which stones were placed to localize the heat. Water applied on either side of the fire prevented its spreading beyond the desired limits. The log so cut off was split with wedges.

Set of Seven Wedges in the End of a Log.

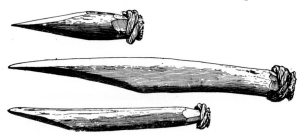

Wedges used for Splitting Boards from Logs.   Kwakiutl.

Among the Kwakiutl seven wedges of graduated lengths, were always set in a row across the end of a log. The longest wedge was the farthest from the workman. With a stone hand-hammer the wedges were tapped in succession until the log was split. It is claimed that the direction of the split along the length of the log was controlled somewhat by manipulating the internal stresses, either by loading the log with stones, or by rolling it until its own weight became effective. Even a small log would furnish several planks of the desired thickness. For some

purposes planks were split radially and for other purposes
with the normal contours of the rings following across the
plank.   The split planks were afterward reduced to the
required thickness and smoothness, with chisels, adzes,
and abrasives.   The chisel was first held at an angle and
driven into the plank; then it was brought down parallel

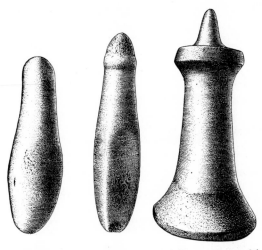

Hand Hammers: Left, for Lateral Blows (Quinault); Right,
for Downward Blows (Kwakiutl).

with the plank and tapped with a hammer, splitting off a
chip, regulated to about four inches in length by the
previous downward cut. A hand adze was employed for
further smoothing. The adzing was either carried along
the length of the plank with the grain, giving a fluted
appearance; or across its width, giving a rippled effect.
If a perfectly smooth surface was desired, grit stones and
shark's skin were employed to remove the adze marks.

Bending Wood. Wood was successfully bent for several purposes. The making of boxes was a particularly ingenious process. A board, split through the heart of the tree, and of a sufficient length to reach around the perimeter of the proposed box, was worked down to a uniform thickness with a chisel and an adze. It was carefully measured with measuring sticks made for the particular purpose, and kerfs were then cut,

Carving Knives and Drill with Bone Point. Kwakiutl.

with the necessary bevel on one side as shown in the illustration. When the board was ready, ditches were dug in the earthen floor of the house, spaced to correspond to the kerfs in the board, which was laid down and hot stones placed below and above the kerfs. Eel grass was then spread over the stones, water poured on, and mats spread over the whole board. When the steam so generated had done its work, wooden clamps, provided for the purpose, were slipped on the board and brought to the edge of the kerf and the board bent to a right angle. When the board had been bent three times, the sides of a square or rectangular box were provided. The board was held in this position by a rope of cedar

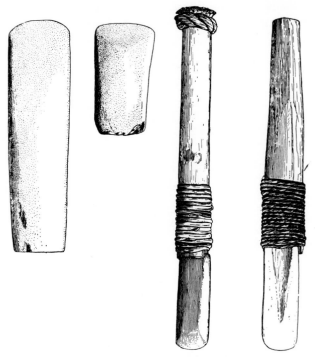

Chisels with Bone Blades.   Kwakiutl.

withes, until diagonal holes had been drilled through the corner, where their ends met.   Wooden pegs were driven into these holes, or spruce root passed through them, to sew the ends together.   A bottom was provided and a groove cut around its edges into which the sides fitted. This bottom was attached to the sides either by pegging or sewing. Many of the boxes were also provided with covers.

Boxes of this sort were used for cooking food by means of hot stones, for water vessels, and for storage. Finally, when death occurred one of the larger boxes was used as a coffin into which the body was placed.

Steaming was also resorted to in producing the abruptly curved fish-hooks used for halibut and cod. Those of the southern tribes were made from the knots

Hand Adze with Stone Blade. Nootka.

where the limbs joined the trunk, worked down to the desired size, and then placed inside a kelp stem. This was buried over night in the hot ashes of the fire. The next morning the pieces were bent to the desired curve and forced into a wooden mold, made by digging a groove with the proper curvature in the surface of a board. When the hooks had set in this mold they were removed, warmed by the fire, rubbed with tallow, and then returned to the mold. The tallow was said to prevent their straightening out in the future.

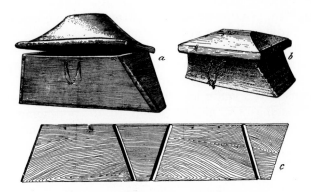

Hunter's Boxes and Board Cut for Folding to Make Such a Box.
Kwakiutl.

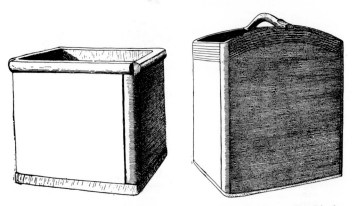

Wooden Vessels: Left, Urinal; Right, Water Bucket. Kwakiutl.

Dugout Dishes. Food-serving dishes were usually made of alder since this wood would not impart a flavor to foods. When a piece of suitable length had been split out, the side nearer the heart of the tree was adzed and shaped for the bottom of the vessel; the outer side was excavated until the sides of the dish were of the required thickness. For feasts very large vessels of this sort were provided, often carved in the form of a person or an animal.

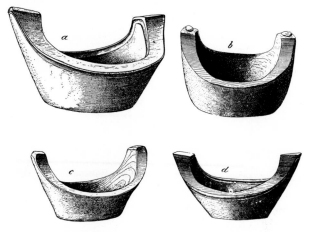

Oil Dishes dug out of Alder.   Kwakiutl.

Canoe-making. The construction of a canoe with primitive tools was a formidable undertaking. When a log of the proper length and size had been secured, the outside was adzed to the approximate shape desired. The inside was excavated, partly by adzing, and partly by the fire which was allowed to char the wood slightly. The charred portion was easily removed and the operation repeated. The thickness of the sides was judged, either by running the hands over the outside and inside and noting irregularities; or by boring holes through the sides, taking measurements and later plugging the holes. The canoe was given a greater width than the diameter of the tree from which it was made, by partially filling it with water which was heated by dropping in hot stones. Cross-pieces were then forced in to spread the canoe which was later held to that shape by thwarts sewed to the gunwales. The stern and bow pieces were made of separate pieces and, sometimes the gunwales were raised by planks, which were sewed on.

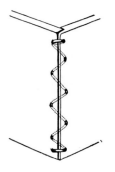

The Joined Corner of Box with Stitching Indicated.   Kwakiutl.

Box with Projection on Lid. Kwakiutl.

Sewing Wood.   Joining wood by sewing must be considered one of the special accomplishments of the Northwest Coast people.   The conception may have been taken over from birchbark work by the interior tribes, but nevertheless great skill was shown in the application of this technique to woodwork.   The spruce root threads were often concealed in deep grooves, so as to be unnoticed in the finished product. Mending of cracks in canoes and other objects was by an ingenious use of sewing.

Superiority in woodwork was further shown by the large timbers and planks which were successfully made and placed in position in house building; by their ingenuity displayed in controlling the cleavage of wood, in bending fish-hooks and box sides; by the technical skill displayed in the adzing; and in the securing by sewing of the large wooden sails formerly used on the canoes.

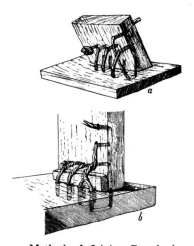

The houses, canoes, vessels for cooking, serving, and storing of food, and the carved poles, are very much in evidence and impress the visitor with the great importance of woodwork in the lives of these people.

Method of Joining Boards by Sewing. Kwakiutl.

BASKETRY AND TEXTILES

The textile products of the Northwest consisted of nets, mats, baskets, and blankets. As in other phases of life, the tribes of the southern and northern portions of the territory may be differentiated from those of the middle sections. In the north, particularly among the Tlingit, basketry and blanket-weaving had a high and very special development.

Nets. Nets were usually made of nettle fiber. The nettles were cut in October and dried for five or six days out-of-doors and then over the house fire. When the stems were thoroughly dry they were somewhat

shredded and the fibers combed out. The women spun
the nettle fiber with the aid of a spindle; the raw
material was draped over a stake, and the fiber, while in
process of spinning, coiled in a box of sand. The
strands were combined and re-combined to produce

Spindle used for Nettle Fibers.   Kwakiutl.

two and four-ply twine, according to the size and
strength required. The net was made by tying the
twine in meshes of uniform size which was determined
by the use of a mesh measure. The long eulachon nets
were conical with a mouth opening about six feet in
diameter, tapering to the smaller end.

Mat Making. The methods of manufacture for
mats as well as the finished products were quite uniform
for the entire area. The material was either the

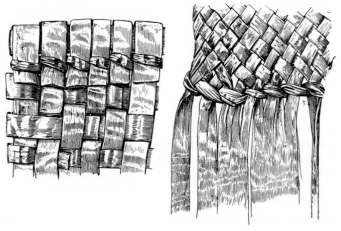

Details of Square and Diagonal Mat Weaving.   Kwakiutl.

inner bark of the red cedar or the much softer bark of
the yellow cedar, varying with the prevalence of the
tree. The cedarbark was divided into strips of ap-
propriate thickness and width and then plaited either
in a plain checker, or diagonally in a
twill. While in progress, the work
was suspended from a bar placed

Twilled Cedarbark Belts.   Kwakiutl.

horizontally at a height convenient for the woman to
work when seated. The warp strands were draped over
this bar so that they hung evenly on either side. To
secure them in position two strands of bark were twined
across the upper edge. If the weaving was to be in

plain checker a weft strand of the same width as the warp was carried across horizontally passing alternately over and under the warp strands. In diagonal weaving the warp and weft strands were interlaced at right angles to each other. The strands removed from the point where the weaving was in progress were tied in bunches to be out of the way. A dish of water was always at hand to keep the material sufficiently damp to be pliable.

In the southern portion of the area along the Fraser River reeds were available for mat making. These were fastened together by passing a string directly through them at intervals.

Carrying straps and narrow bands were also made in the diagonal plaiting technique, the strands being bent over at the edges and continuing at right angles to their previous course. Little decoration was attempted in work of this sort, but darker strands were sometimes introduced to produce diagonal patterns. The direction of the twilling was also sometimes changed so that lines forming right angles were produced. Baskets and bags were made of similar material and by the same method. After a square bottom was plaited it was suspended by strings from the four corners so that the bottom was in a horizontal position and the ends of the strands hung down. The weaving then proceeded around the basket until the walls were of the required height.

Basketry. For certain types of basket the prevailing technique was in open work twining. Warp strands, usually of split spruce root, were interwoven in checker work to form the bottom and were then continued upward to serve only as a warp. The weft consisted of two sets of smaller and more pliable root material. One of these was placed horizontally along the inside of the basket and the second wrapped around the first between each warp strand and then carried outside the warp strand diagonally, firmly binding the two together. Such baskets are of open-work and the weft strands are spaced so as to give the desired openness. A basket of very pleasing appearance was produced by arranging the warp strands so that they run diagonally up the basket in opposite directions

Bag illustrating Open-twining. Kwakiutl.

Details of Tlingit Basketry; Top, Two-strand Twining; Bottom, Three-strand Twining.

so as to cross. Two strands of the same material are twined around horizontally engaging these warp strands. *Tlingit Baskets.* The northern Tlingit have developed a great variety of ornamented baskets of twined weave. The material employed by the Tlingit in constructing these baskets was obtained from the smaller roots of the Sitka spruce. As soon as the roots

Spruce Root Hat with Cedarbark Cover.   Kwakiutl.

Spruce Root Basket, Bird-cage (Openwork Twine) Stitch (above) and Double Basket of Checkerwork (below).   Kwakiutl

Berrying Basket with Carrying Strap and a Carrying Strap used by Mountain Goat Hunters. Kwakiutl.

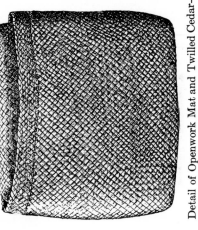

Detail of Openwork Mat and Twilled Cedarbark Pouch. Kwakiutl.

Tlingit Baskets.

were gathered the bark was removed by carefully roasting the roots and pulling them through a split stick.
The roots were then divided: the outer portions, smooth
and shiny, were used for the weft, the inner layers for
the warp; the hearts were discarded. These roots
were gathered in the spring or summer and seasoned
until winter which was the proper time for basket-
making. Three kinds of twining were employed:
plain two-strand twining; three-strand twining when
strength was desired at the turn of the basket where
the walls begin; and two-strand twining over pairs of
warp strands, which were re-grouped in the succeeding
rows to give a diagonal effect.

The ornamentation was produced by over-laying
the weft with grass or maiden-hair fern stems. The
grass was either bleached and used white or dyed. The
material was dyed black by burying it for a time in
certain types of black mud or by steeping it in an in-
fusion of hemlock bark. Yellow dye, made from tree
moss or from the roots of Oregon grape was also
employed, as well as red from an alder vessel in which
urine had been allowed to stand. A purple was produced from huckleberries. Like nearly all textile
designs these naturally resulted in geometrical patterns.
Esthetically, these are among the most pleasing of
North American Indian baskets. The technical execu-
tion is excellent, the colors harmonize, and spacing is
nicely arranged. Formerly, they were made for household use; for cooking, for water, and for storing food,
varying in size and form according to these requirements.

Cedarbark Blankets. The Kwakiutl wove blankets
and capes of fiber made from the bark of the cedar.
The inner bark was taken from the tree in July
and soaked for ten days by weighing it down in still,
shallow, salt water. It was then beaten across the

grain by an implement, made from the bone of a whale, in shape and appearance like the Polynesian tapa beaters. For weaving, a frame was erected, consisting of two stakes set up vertically at the required distance from each other to the top of which was tied a horizontal bar, provided with a groove on its lower edge. A strip of cedarbark was then fastened to the two stakes

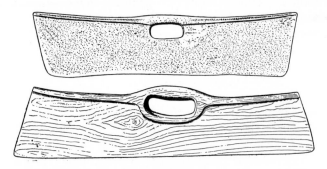

Implements for shredding Cedarbark. Upper, of Bone of Whale; Lower, of Wood. Kwakiutl.

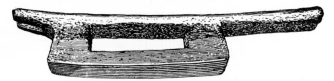

Beater for Cedarbark. Kwakiutl.

and attached just under the horizontal bar. The warp of soft cedarbark was draped over this line which was then pressed into the groove in the horizontal bar and bound tightly in place. The warp fibers were separated into small units, each of which became a warp strand. The weft consisted of two strands which were twined across horizontally. The blankets and capes were given the desired shapes by inclining the tops of the posts toward each other, and, by making the warp strands in the middle longer than those at the two edges. Yarn of mountain goat wool was used for the border of these fabrics which in earlier days were also bound with strips of sea-otter fur.

Chilkat Blankets. The Chilkat of Lynn Canal carried the weaving of mountain goat wool to a very high development. The skins of three animals were required to give sufficient wool for one blanket. The skins

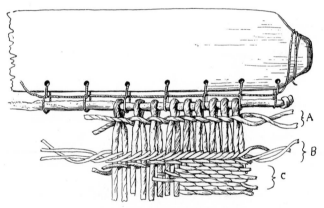

Detail of suspending a Chilkat Blanket.

were soaked until the wool and hair loosened and could be easily pulled off. The coarse hair was discarded and the wool spun between the palm of the hand and the thigh. Two-strand yarn was made for the weft. The warp was prepared by enclosing a strand of cedarbark with a strand of goat wool yarn. Three colors were employed in dyeing yarn for the weft: Black was obtained from hemlock bark and yellow from the tree moss, *Evernia vulpina.* Decoctions were made of these in urine and the wool boiled in them for some hours and

allowed to steep much longer.   A green blue was secured
by allowing copper to corrode in urine and boiling wool
in the resulting liquid.

   The loom was similar to that used for weaving the
cedarbark blankets described above.   The posts,
however, were placed in heavy wooden blocks instead of
in the ground.   The warp strands were cut in several
lengths and then sorted and arranged to give the finished
blanket the desired curve at the bottom.   The long

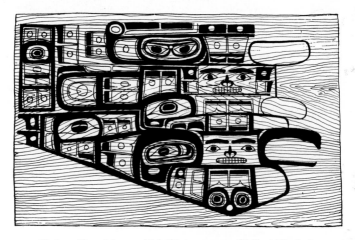

Pattern Board from which Women weave Chilkat Blankets.

warp strands of a newly commenced blanket were
gathered in bundles and placed in bags to keep them
out of the way and also to keep them clean.   Simple
two-strand twining was first employed and then three-
strand twining.   In the body of the blanket two-strand
twining was so manipulated as to produce a diagonal
effect.   This is accomplished by including two warp
strands between each twist and the crossing of the weft
strands, and the next time pairing the warp strands

differently. The colored weft strand was not carried entirely across the web, but only to the edge of a unit of the pattern. The designs were composed of the usual conventionalized and semi-religious motives of the region. Since the women were not supposed to be familiar with them they were drawn on a board by some man. The blankets being nearly always bilaterally symmetrical, it was considered sufficient to draw the pattern to include only the middle and one side of the board. While these blankets were woven only

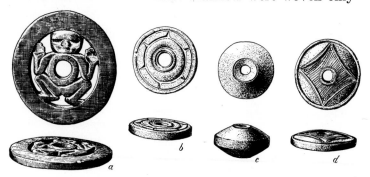

Spindle Whorls.

by the Chilkat, at least in modern times, they are possessed as objects of wealth by most Northwest Coast tribes and worn on ceremonial occasions.

Salish Blankets. The Salish peoples of the south, particularly on the lower Fraser River, made blankets of a type quite different from those of the Tlingit. In addition to the mountain goat wool they had a supply derived from white woolly dogs bred for the purpose. The wool was mixed with diatomaceous earth and beaten to remove the grease and make the fibers adhere more readily in the spinning, which was done between the palm of the hand and the thigh. The spun threads

were twisted into two-strand yarn with the aid of a
spindle which had a large decorated whorl. To secure
the desired tension, the threads were drawn over a
beam or other handy object. Feathers were also
combined with the wool in spinning. The loom consisted of two uprights into which two horizontal rollers
were fitted. By the use of uprights of varying heights,
a web of any desired size could be made. The rollers
were wedged apart to give the needed tension to the
warp. The warp threads were not carried spirally
around the two rollers, but were passed around a
tightly drawn cord or a stick and then doubled back so
that when the web was finished and the cord or stick
withdrawn, the fabric would separate into a single
piece with four selvages. When weaving, the woman
sat in front of the loom with a ball of weft which she
passed through the shed, beating it down with a comb.
As the work progressed she drew the warp around the
rollers after loosening the wedges which held them in
place. In weaving the warp strands were usually
grouped in pairs, producing a diagonal appearance.
Occasionally ornamentation was attempted by the use
of color, black or brown, introduced as stripes into the
warp. The diagonal treatment then produced narrow
bands broken with alternate white and colored lines
having an upward and downward slope.

Food Gathering

Probably no region of the world excelled the Northwest Coast in abundance and variety of marine life.
It was largely from this source that the tribes of this
area derived their food supply. At certain seasons of
the year the sea and rivers literally teem with salmon
and this fish was the staple article of diet, corresponding
in that respect to maize among the Pueblo tribes or to

buffalo among the Indians of the Plains. Other species of fish, as well as shellfish and sea mammals occur in great abundance throughout the area, but these were of lesser importance in the dietary of these people. Further variety in foodstuffs was supplied by land mammals and by such plant foods as berries, roots, and barks. These almost limitless supplies of food resulted in a complete absence of periods of famine. The comparative ease with which it was possible to secure an adequate supply of food during a few months of the year probably accounts for the exuberance of the ceremonial life during the somewhat idle winter months.

Whaling. The food of the people of the Northwest Coast was chiefly drawn from the sea, but again distinction may be made between the various portions of the area. The Nootka, of the southern section, had one outstanding achievement not common to the other tribes. They and some of their neighbors to the south pursued and killed whales, while the northern tribes were content with those which were stranded or cast up on the beach. Usually it was the California gray whale which was taken. The chief harpooner was a man of distinction, who inherited the position, and was under many restrictions regarding his food and social behavior. In particular, at the proper season he withdrew to a certain "house" consisting only of posts and poles and not enclosed or covered with planks. In this were many wooden figures of men and the skulls of his ancestors. Here he kept his vigils and engaged in prayer for success. The equipment for whaling consisted of canoes capable of accommodating eight men and sufficiently sturdy to be taken well outside the sheltered inlets. The harpoons had a head with a broad triangular metal or shell blade, antler barbs, and a shaft of yew wood ten feet long, tapering from the middle toward each end. The lines consisted of a leader of whale sinew and sections of rope made from cedar withes. Floats were attached. The outer end of the shaft was inserted in the harpoon head which became detached as soon as the whale was struck.

The harpooner aimed at a spot just behind the front flipper of the whale. As soon as the whale was struck, the crews of the other canoes were permitted to throw as many harpoons as possible. The movements of the whale were impeded by the many attached sealskin floats and he was readily dispatched with lances. The floats, sometimes forty to fifty in number, prevented

Float made of Seal Bladder. Kwakiutl.

the sinking of the dead whale which was towed to a beach at or near the village. The "whale chief," who threw the first harpoon, was entitled to a piece of blubber from the back between the head and the dorsal fin. This was decorated with feathers and supported by two stakes and a cross-piece until such time as it was convenient to have a feast. The remainder of the whale was cut up and distributed, the blubber being divided into sections about two feet square. Practically the entire animal was consumed or utilized in some way. The black skin was eaten, the sinews used for ropes, and the digestive organs employed as containers for oil. The Nootka, as well as the other tribes who did not pursue whales, gladly made use of any animal which was stranded on the shore. The Nootka took sea-lions in a manner similar to that described above for whaling. Harpooning sea-lions was an inherited duty, the position of harpooner being second in honor to that of the chief.

Hunting Porpoises. Porpoises were taken with a harpoon. The Kwakiutl used a special canoe made and afterward kept as smooth as possible, and never dragged on the ground or allowed to grate on the shore. It was greased with tallow and scented with spruce boughs. The crew consisted of a steersman and a harpooner who directed the operations, communicating with the steersman by signs. Great care was taken to make no noise in paddling. The harpoon was two-pronged, with detachable barbed heads, fastened to a long line. A float was attached to the line. When a porpoise had been approached within striking distance, a harpoon was thrown, and the canoe backed to avoid the wounded animal, which dove and rose again near the same spot. The canoe was then brought close to the animal which was thrust through the body with a harpoon handle or a long lance. Usually several canoes engaged in such a hunt encircled the victim.

Sealing. Seals were hunted in much the same manner as porpoises. Great care was exercised after harpooning to prevent the seal from swimming through kelp or seaweed and entangling the line which would

Harpoon for Salmon: a″ Shows Detached Head. Kwakiutl.

then be broken or pulled loose. The hunters continually drove him under water with the harpoon pole until the animal was nearly or quite drowned. A blow with a club finished him. The seal hunters knew where the seals customarily slept. When the seals took to the water, the harpooner thrust into the phosphorescence under the water and secured the seal before he had time to escape. Seal meat was highly prized and much used in the feasts.

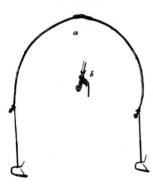

Halibut Hooks set in Pairs. Kwakiutl.

Fishing. Many varieties of fish flourished in the ocean and its inlets. Chief among these were the halibut, cod, herring, salmon, and eulachon. The particular local conditions determined which of these fish held the first place as food. In certain regions the halibut was of special importance. There are excellent banks in Queen Charlotte Sound and in Dixon Entrance, north of the Queen Charlotte Islands. The Haida and Kwakiutl, therefore, made great use of halibut. The method of taking these fish was everywhere the same. Large hooks were used, those of the Kwakiutl having been constructed by bending a fir or hemlock stick as described above. Farther north, a V-shaped hook was made, and ornamented by carving. A barb of sharp bone or antler was baited with a piece of squid. The hook was attached to a line made of twisted kelp stem, about one-quarter of an inch in diameter, and very strong when wet. The other end of the line was attached to a float; and a sinker rested on the bottom, steadying the hook and holding it in a vertical position. The Kwakiutl were accustomed to set these hooks in pairs so that only one sinker and one float were required for the two hooks. When the huge fish took the bait, the outer curves or prongs of the hook passed outside of its mouth and served 'as a lever to drive the barb deep into its flesh. In the accounts of the earlier voyages, great praise is given to this device which the white seamen themselves adopted with profit.

The fish were cleaned on the shore by the women, who cut off the heads and tails for separate treatment. The skin was also removed and dried separately from the flesh which was thinly sliced for drying. The heads and tails were cooked by boiling and steaming, and the dried skin toasted over the fire, while the dried white flesh was dipped in oil and eaten raw.

Cod and kelp fish were also taken with a line, anchored in a horizontal position near the bottom, to which a number of baited hooks were attached. Some of the Kwakiutl fastened the sinkers so that they were detached before the line was pulled up, saving the exertion of drawing them to the surface.

For many of the Northwest Coast tribes salmon supplied a large proportion of the food. They were formerly taken by a number of methods. Trolling was practised with a straight hook provided with a sharp barb placed at an acute angle. The baited hook trailed on the end of a line which the fisherman held in his hand as he paddled. The motion thus imparted to the hook simulated the movement of a live fish and attracted the salmon.

Where the condition of the water permitted, a two-pronged spear, similar to the one employed in harpooning porpoises, was employed. Long nets were formerly use by the Salish who lived near Victoria. Nets

Dam and Fish Trap.   Kwakiutl.

Dam and Fish Basket for Salmon.   Kwakiutl.

were woven from nettle fiber twine. When the salmon run began, the chief who owned a fishing place invited his relatives to join him for the season. During the season the men were divided into two groups, living with their families on either side of the salmon drying racks. The chief's quarters were at the end of these racks, opposite the water. From these two groups were chosen the crews for the canoes employed in fishing.

Trolling Hook for Salmon and Clubs for killing Halibut. Kwakiutl.

Two anchors of large stones were placed at a distance from each other equal to the length of the net. Buoys were attached to the anchors and the canoes moored to them during the fishing. The net was stretched between the canoes until it was full of fish, when the canoes were brought toward each other, the net was pulled in. Nets were also used by the other tribes especially in the rivers, where they were stretched between two canoes

Salmon Trap for Narrow Streams.   Kwakiutl.

Weir for Eulachon Fishing.   Kwakiutl.

by means of which they were drawn down with the current or against the flow of the tide. These were either gill nets, in which the fish were caught when they tried to pass through; or they were provided with trailing pockets, into which the salmon passed.

The commonest method of taking salmon was by means of a weir across or at the sides of a stream, associated with which were fish baskets for collecting the fish or an advantageous place for spearing them. Because of the variations in the size, depth, and swiftness of the streams, there were many forms of these weirs and traps, adapted to the particular localities where they were used. The character of some of these will be readily observed in the illustrations.

In shallow rivers, such as the Nimkish in the Kwakiutl territory, and the Chilkat River of the Tlingit area, dog salmon were easily secured by means of a hook attached to a long pole. The hook was drawn along the bottom toward the canoe in which the fisherman stood. This method of fishing was pursued at night, unless the river was sufficiently roily, as is the case with the Chilkat River, so that the salmon do not see the fisherman. The fish themselves were so numerous that it was not necessary that the fishermen see them. Along the rivers were suitable places for fishing from a platform extending from the bank over a pool or eddy. The fisherman used either a net, a gaff hook, or a harpoon. Such favorable fishing sites were highly prized possessions.

The women received the salmon at the shore and prepared them for curing. The heads, tails, and fins were removed and the fish split down the back. The heads and tails were boiled or steamed and eaten fresh, while the sliced bodies and the roe were hung on poles to dry in the smoke of the fires.

Another fish of great importance in the life of the northwestern people, was the eulachon. These fish are rather small, nine to twelve inches long, but they arrive at the mouths of certain rivers in great multitudes. The Nass River, in the Tsimshian country, is the most noted fishery for eulachon. The first arrivals are in the middle of March and the fish continue to run

Salmon Drying. Chilkat River, Alaska.

for about six weeks. As the fish come up to the mouth of the river, they are pursued by seals, sea-lions, and whales; and while in the river, great flocks of seagulls appear every day and feed upon them until night.

Piles were driven deep into the stream bed with stone pile drivers. Sliding on these posts were rings to which the net was attached. The lower rings were pushed to the bottom of the river with a pole when the net was open for use. The nets were long, bag-shaped, with wide mouths. While the ice from the upper river was running out, fishing was difficult, for the nets were liable to be carried away; and canoe navigation in the running ice was hazardous. After the ice had disappeared the nets had to be opened anew at every tide.

The oil from the fish used to be tried out by placing hot rocks in large wooden vessels, or canoes, thus keeping the water boiling until the oil from the fish gathered on the surface, where it was recovered after it cooled. After boiling, the fish were pressed, to force out the remaining oil. Formerly, the women accomplished this by squeezing the still hot fish against their naked breasts. The accumulations resulting from this process were not allowed to be wiped off until the season was over. Nowadays, the oil is rendered in home-made furnaces of sheet metal under which fires can be maintained and presses with levers are provided for extracting the oil. It was customary to allow the fish to decay somewhat before submitting them to this process, since the oil was then more easily separated, and the Indians are not prejudiced against the odor or taste of slightly putrid fish oil.

Eulachon oil was highly prized; dried salmon, halibut, and other foods were dipped into it and formed a favorite sauce for such dishes as dried berries and smoked meats. Trade in eulachon oil was formerly very extensive. Indians from a distance came to the favorable fishing places and bought temporary rights to fish and render the oil. Long trails, known as "grease trails," led into the interior, where the coast people traded with the Athaspascan-speaking tribes. The oil was carried by canoe and also traded among the Northwest Coast people. It does not deteriorate with time and may, therefore, be stored for a year or two. This

Eulachon or Candlefish in Storage.

Rendering Eulachon Oil in a Canoe by Means of Hot Stones.

was fortunate for great runs of eulachon do not occur every year.

The spawn of herring was collected for food, usually by anchoring quantities of cedar or hemlock brush in

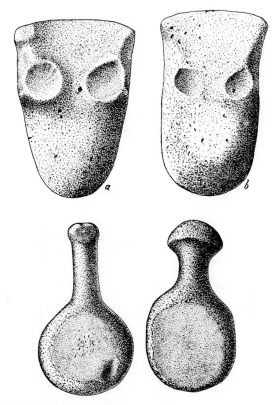

Pile Drivers: a and b, Bella Coola; Lower Pair, Quinault.

the spawning places. When the brush was withdrawn it was covered with a mass of eggs. The Tlingit and Tsimshian gathered the seaweed on which the herring

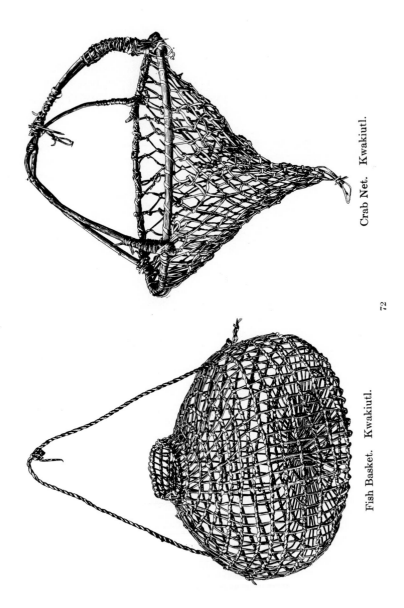

Crab Net.   Kwakiutl.

Fish Basket.   Kwakiutl.

spawned. The herring themselves were secured with a rake, a stick with a row of sharp pieces of bone set in one side; but in more recent times, nails replaced the bone spikes. The fisherman sat in the stern of the canoe while his wife paddled in the bow, driving the canoe astern. The rake was swung edgewise through the water, the fish being impaled on the points and shaken off into the canoe. Eulachon were also taken in this manner. In early spring, herring were driven to the coast in numbers so great that they could scarcely find room in the shallow water.

Herring Rake.   Kwakiutl.

Shellfish. Beside these major products of the sea certain minor ones such as shellfish are of considerable importance. The Haida classed these together as low tide foods and under certain circumstances they were under taboo. There are two important species of clams. The more common one is of ordinary size and fairly abundant. It was the woman's duty to dig them, in former times, with a digging-stick and a large shell. In transporting them she protected herself from the salt water, by placing a mat on her back under the carrying basket. For immediate use these clams were roasted over a fire, or steam-cooked in a box. When larger quantities were prepared for future use, they were steamed under a covering of seaweeds and mats. In this case, the clams were removed from the shells and strung on sticks or a strand of bark. These were exposed for some time to the heat of a fire and then smoked until they were thoroughly cured.

The large horse clam was also used for food. The
shells of these are eight or ten inches in length. They
were secured with some difficulty, as the clams are
capable of descending into the sand with considerable
speed. These were cooked by steaming and because of
their size were strung on three sticks. They were
then exposed to fire and smoke as were the smaller
clams. Cockles, mussels, and many other forms of
sea life contributed to the food supply which was so
abundant that famine was practically unknown among
the tribes living directly on the coast.

Digging-sticks. Kwakiutl.

Vegetable Food. The vegetable diet of the Indians
on the Northwest Coast was quite varied, but not
particularly abundant. They did not practise agriculture as did some of the Indians east of the Rocky
Mountains in the United States, nor did they have
acorns in abundance as in California. From the sea
they took eelgrass and seaweed. They utilized fern
and bracken, and clover roots. They had a fair variety
of wild fruits including elderberries, huckleberries,
salmon berries, gooseberries, rose hips, salal berries,
and crab-apples. The roots were cooked by steaming in
underground ovens or were roasted on the coals and
eaten with oil. The seaweed was allowed to decay a
little before being dried and stored for winter use.
The dried weed was chopped up with an adze and
chewed before being boiled and served in oil. The
berries were usually cooked, dried, and stored in cakes

for future use. These were soaked in water, broken up, kneaded until soft, covered with oil, and eaten with a spoon. Huckleberries were boiled with salmon spawn and packed in wooden boxes sealed with eulachon fat. Wild crab-apples served with oil were a favorite dish. Starches, except in the south, were poorly represented, and were found chiefly in the form of camass bulbs. In southern British Columbia and in Washington and Oregon the camass is plentiful. It was cooked in quantities in underground ovens and provided excellent and palatable food. Wild seeds and grains so much

Tongs: Lower Two are sharpened for Thrusting into the Ground When used for Roasting. Kwakiutl.

used in California and the Great Basin were little used on the Northwest Coast. In the spring quantities of the inner bark, cambium layer, of the hemlock were removed and stored for winter use.

The clover roots mentioned above were secured from "clover gardens" situated on low ground where a wild clover grows abundantly. These gardens were family property which could not be sold nor given away, but descended in the family by inheritance. The clover roots were dug in the autumn after the leaves of the trees had fallen. Pebbles were removed and roots unsuitable for food were sometimes replanted, but otherwise the plots were not cultivated by the owner.

Bird Spear.   Nootka.

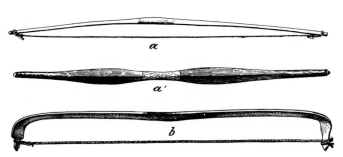

a

a'

b

Bows.   Kwakiutl.

Arrows: a, for Birds; c, and d, for Sea-otter.   Kwakiutl.

Tobacco. Though the tribes of this region were characterized above as non-agricultural, tobacco was cultivated, as was the case in California and certain sections of the Great Plains. The tobacco (*Nicotiana attenuata*) was grown in small gardens near the villages. Especially among the northern tribes of the area, it seems not to have been smoked, however, in pre-European times, but was chewed with lime. The dried leaves and stems were reduced to a powder in small stone mortars. Small portions of the powder were placed in the mouth to which quick-lime obtained by burning clam shells was added with a stick. It is quite remarkable that the habit of smoking, so nearly universal in aboriginal America, should not have obtained save in the southern part of the Northwest Coast area.

The cultivation of potatoes was introduced in the period of the early voyages by explorers and traders, and quickly spread wherever conditions were favorable.

Land Animals. As has been previously stated, the people of the Northwest Coast secured the greater part of their food supply from the ocean and only a minor portion by the hunting of land mammals. Deer were taken either in snares or shot with bow and arrow. The Nootka had certain restrictions regarding the eating of deer and fish during the same season. Bears killed in deadfalls were given a ceremonial welcome and feast. Eating bear meat also involved a taboo against salmon.

Mountain goats were frequently hunted by the mainland tribes. They did not occur on the islands. Nooses were set in the trails where there was a sheer wall above and below so that the trail must be used. The goats were also run with dogs and when cornered or brought to bay were taken by dropping a noose over their heads. The wool was much prized for the making

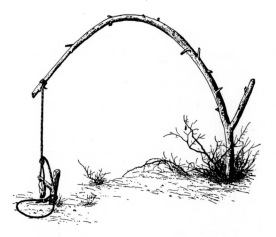

Spring Trap used for Bear, Deer, and Smaller Animals. Kwakiutl.

Deadfalls. Kwakiutl.

of blankets. The flesh was eaten fresh or cured with smoke and in the sun, and stored away in large quantities for future use.

DRESS AND DECORATION

The mild climate of the Northwest Coast made warm clothing unnecessary and the damp weather was a factor which militated against the use of skins for clothing. Consequently, we find the tribes of this area wearing a minimum amount of clothing. The men went about entirely nude during the summer months and the women wore only a grass skirt closely resembling that worn in Polynesia. Clothing was worn as a protection against rain rather than against cold. Leather garments are of small value in a wet climate and we find the tribes of this area employing instead clothing of vegetable fiber.

Footgear. One of the striking features of the Northwest Coast costume, distinguishing it from the remainder of North America, is the almost total lack of footwear. In Mexico, Arizona, and southern California, sandals were worn, protecting the feet, not against the cold, but against the hard surface of the ground. East and west of the Rocky Mountains almost to the coast, moccasins of some sort were worn. Moccasins in the Eastern Woodland area were made in one piece, with soft soles, but throughout the Plains region, in two pieces with hard soles, more adaptable to the dry, hard trails. Except in the far north and in the interior, the Northwest Coast people were bare-legged and bare-footed, summer and winter. They were unaccustomed to extensive land travel and, therefore, needed less protection for their feet than did the Indians living inland. The cold months are also wet

Woman's Apron.　Kwakiutl.

Ornaments: a, Anklet; b, Bracelet.

Hair Ornament of Dentalium
Shells.　Kwakiutl.

months and untanned leather soon became water-soaked and of doubtful value as foot covering.

Men's Clothing. The men of the Coast were accustomed to go about in summer entirely devoid of clothing. For ceremonial occasions and in winter a rectangular robe of skins or woven fiber was wrapped around the body under the left arm and over the right shoulder, hanging to the knees. When Europeans first visited the coast, many of these robes were made of sea-otter skin and their purchase from the backs of the people inaugurated the fur trade of that coast.

Hat on which Whale Hunting is depicted. Nootka.

Waterproof mats, cut like a poncho, were worn by both men and women in wet weather.

The beard was eradicated, except by some of the older men; the hair was worn long, loose, or bunched on top of the head. Slaves were compelled to wear their hair short. Hats were worn only as a protection against the rain. On dress occasions especially, the body and face were coated with oil over which red ocher, mica, and sparkling sand were applied. On all religious occasions, white down was strewed over the hair. Down was a symbol of peace and goodwill and its use is often mentioned in the early accounts. The men were very fond of ear and nose pendants, using twigs of cedar, feathers, pieces of wood and bone, and, when they could be secured, metal objects of all descriptions.

Women's Dress. The woman wore aprons of shredded
bark tied around the waist and reaching the knees.
Except on rare ceremonial occasions, this garment was
not laid aside in public. Ordinarily, the women also
wore a cedarbark garment which covered them from
the shoulders, where it was fastened about the neck,
to the ankles. A girdle was worn with this, confining
the garment to the waist; they also wore tight bands
about the ankles, as well as bracelets, nose, and earrings. In the north, the Tsimshian, Haida, and

Cradle with Cedarbark Bedding. Kwakiutl.

Tlingit women slit their lower lips and inserted a wooden
plug. This opening was increased in size according to
her age and rank so that the lip plug or labret of grooved
wood might ultimately measure three by four inches.
This held her lip in a horizontal position as long as she
wore it; otherwise the lip drooped down on her chin.

Tattooing. As was usual in America, tattooing was
generally practised by both sexes. The pigment was
introduced by rubbing carbon in the form of soot under
the skin, resulting in a blue color. The tattooing was
chiefly applied to the front of the legs and back of the

arms, and less frequently to the chest. The designs, representing inherited crests, were in the symmetrical conventional style used in painting.

Deformed Heads. Two types of head deformation were practised on the Pacific Coast. In Washington and northward among the related Salish of British Columbia, the forehead was flattened so that the head sloped back from the eyes to a summit at the back. Since this treatment was not permitted for the slaves, an undeformed head indicated a freeman. Just north of the area where head flattening was practised, another style prevailed among the Kwakiutl. The top of the head was bound so as to decrease its diameter and elongate it upward and backward.

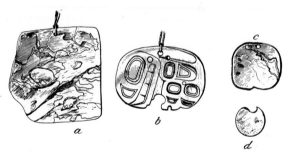

Nose Ornaments of Abalone Shell. Kwakiutl.

Kwakiutl Woman with Deformed Head.

CHAPTER III

SOCIAL AND POLITICAL ORGANIZATION

SOCIAL DISTINCTIONS

In preceding sections there has been repeated mention of such groups as the Haida, Tlingit, Kwakiutl, etc. Actually, these are not single tribes, but linguistic groups, each of which consists of a number of tribes which are further divided into sub-tribes. Each of these sub-tribes may, in turn, consist of a number of village groups. Actually, it was these village groups which were the basic social units of the Northwest Coast· people.

In addition, the Tlingit, Haida, and Tsimshian had certain artificial social divisions, membership in which depended upon descent through the mother. These groups were known as clans, and one belonged to the same clan as his mother. Among the Kwakiutl groups, the Bella Coola, and certain other tribes, there was a curious division into septs. South of the Kwakiutl the tribes were simply organized on the basis of village groups.

The Indians of the Northwest Coast differ from the other natives of North America in the amount of emphasis they place upon wealth and property and upon the ceremonial distribution of wealth. Closely linked with this was the concept of an aristocracy of blood. In each village group there tended to be one to several families of wealth and distinction and of aristocratic blood who consequently dominated within the village in which they resided. Since there is a tendency for these aristocratic families to intermarry, the lineage groups or aristocratic families were closely interbred and formed a group apart throughout the entire tribe.

Below this "nobility" of wealth and lineage was a second group of persons less wealthy or less closely related to the dominating families; they were the poor relations of the nobility, the general run of the population. Below these was the third and last class, the slaves. These were captives taken in war or such captives purchased from other tribes together with their descendants.

To be rich meant to be well born and conversely to be well born usually meant that a man was wealthy. Wealth was not held so much for wealth's sake, but rather its possession enabled a man to show the greatness of his family. This he did by making ceremonial distributions of this wealth at stated intervals or for certain occasions. In this way he exhalted the honor of his family and indicated his wealth was so great that he could distribute or destroy it with impunity.

Below the wealthy chiefs the social classes graded downward without formal rankings. First, were those closely related to the high born chiefs; below these, others less closely related; and further down the scale, the poor relations of the chiefs who were usually hangers-on at their households. There was also a rather illy-defined middle class who, while not of high birth, possessed some worldly goods. It was sometimes possible for a member of this class to rise somewhat in the social scale through the accumulation of wealth. Usually this made it possible for a man to marry a child into a family of higher rank, thereby raising himself in the esteem of his fellow tribesmen. Below this median stratum, and at the bottom of the social scale, were the slaves. Slavery was known among nearly all of the tribes of North America, but the slaves were usually war captives who were adopted into the tribe and consequently suffered few if any social disabilities. However, on the Northwest Coast where there was so strong a development of a sense of aristocracy and wealth, slaves were held as mere chattels and both they and their descendants remained slaves and were regarded as being merely a form of property to be traded, given away, or killed, to enhance the prestige of their masters. A slave or a descendant of a slave could not rise above his social class.

Septs. Over the greater part of the Northwest Coast there were groups of considerable size, the members of which considered themselves related at least to the extent of being descended from the same "first ancestors." Thus, they might be likened to the several branches of a family line. These extended families, or septs, were distinguished by names which served as do our surnames in holding their members together. Theoretically, all chiefs were merely heads of such extended families, but the chiefs differed in rank so that the head of the family of the highest rank in the sept, was chief of the sept. The chief of the sept ranking the highest in the village was the chief of the village.

Just as there were varying but definite gradations of rank among the common people, so the chiefs were definitely graded. Among the Kwakiutl this grading of the chiefs was mainly, or perhaps entirely on the theory of primogeniture. The oldest son was the head of the house; the oldest son in the line of the oldest sons in the sept, village, and group held the headship in each. This was not necessarily the real origin of the order of rank, but the Kwakiutl were accustomed to interpret social distinctions in this manner. In this estimate of worth and standing, the mother as well as the father was considered; therefore, a chief strove to marry as high in rank as possible and thereby elevated the position of his descendants. If he married beneath his rank he lowered the position of his family and such a blot was remembered from generation to generation. In reality, this may have been the native way of explaining that certain families were less highly esteemed than others.

Chiefs. As has been stated, at the top of the social pyramid were the chiefs and those so close to them that they had a kind of reflected glory. In principle, the chief differed only in degree from the lesser individuals. Like them, he inherited a named house, together with the right to decorate it with certain carvings and paintings; a number of feast dishes with names for them, as well as names for his canoes; certain traditional names for himself and the members of his family; family origin myths which were publicly dramatized; and other dignities. In addition, he inherited the duty of controlling the social unit of which he was the head.

Rivalry of Chiefs. While it is probable that the relative order of ranking for the chiefs was stable from generation to generation, constant attempts were made by them to increase their prestige at the expense of their rivals. In this rivalry, they resorted to methods similar to those employed by the common people to secure their advancement. In connection with the same events in family life, birth, puberty, marriage, and death, the chiefs distributed property and gave feasts, and carried them out on a still greater scale. In addition to these general ceremonies, the chiefs sought opportunities for outdoing their rivals and putting them to shame. One form of rivalry among the Kwakiutl was to give an "oil feast" during which the eulachon oil was served with other food and great quantities of the precious fluid were thrown upon the fire, or allowed to flow on to it from above. The flames leapt up and often set the roof of the house on fire. The guest, who was the rival, had to retain his seat near the fire, keeping his composure until the host gave the order to abate the flames, and extinguish the fire which was burning the house above them. However, if the guest believed that he had not been outdone; that at some time he himself had given a greater feast, he was privileged to refuse to accept the proffered spoon of oil and went to his house to bring a "copper" which he broke and gave to his host, and thus "put out the fire." Not to be outdone, the host, in his absence, had to attach a copper to each of the four house posts. If beaten, the guest was "shamed," and soon was under obligation to give a greater feast to remove the smirch on his reputation.

A Copper: Design, Horned Owl.

Another form of rivalry consisted in breaking up coppers. The coppers were shield-shaped with a rib running across the middle and from the center to one end. They were of native manufacture, the older ones being made of metal found in a free state near Copper River. Each had a name and a well-known history and its value depended on this history and the amount for which it had been sold. One chief broke a copper of well-known value and gave the pieces to his rival who was compelled to destroy a copper of equal or greater value and give in return the parts of both, or lose in prestige. A more extreme act was to break a copper and throw

A Chief with his Broken Copper.   Kwakiutl.

the parts into the sea. Canoes were also sunk and slaves killed.

These property contests generally occurred between chiefs who were traditional rivals. They may have been chiefs of septs or of villages, or the leaders of more remote groups. In all of these contests the chief acted for the members of his group who contributed very largely to the property used. It is certain also that for some of the peoples of the Northwest Coast the chief had a symbolic relation to his group, so that there was an emotional transfer to him of its power and prestige. If he succeeded in raising his rank, he carried the group up with him. If he suffered insult, the group was correspondingly put to shame.

Feasts. In addition to serving as a weapon in social rivalry, accumulated wealth was also distributed in more purely social feasts. Practically every social event required the giving of a feast which in turn necessitated a proper house and an ample supply of food. Every such event also required the distribution of property, some of it was in payment for services rendered, but much of it was bestowed on the guests of the occasion, according to their rank. The events requiring feasts were the naming of a child; the puberty of girls and at that time the piercing of the ears, and nose, and the lower lip for the labret; the tattooing of both sexes; the burial of a relative; the building of a house; and the assumption of a predecessor's position and rank. The relative importance of the events varied according to the tribe. The Nootka placed the puberty ceremony first while the Tlingit and Haida held in highest esteem the ceremony attending the final placing of the remains of a deceased relative. Whenever one of these events occurred, the person who gave the ceremony assumed a new name, and displayed by carvings, paintings, or,

more generally, by dramatic representation, one or
more of his inherited honors.

A man's renown was increased according to the fre-
quency of the celebrations and the lavishness with
which they were carried out. In order to give them at
all, he must have inherited or acquired certain names
and honors which he could publicly assume or display.
The inherited names or honors came from his father's
or mother's line, according to the tribal rules of inheritance. Among the Nootka they were inherited
from either father or mother, with the Kwakiutl some
of them always descended from the father to the eldest
child; among the Bella Coola they were willed, according to a fixed rule; while among the northern tribes the
more important ones passed from a man to his sister's
son. Names and honors or crests particularly among the
Kwakiutl were secured through marriage. The father-
in-law bestowed these upon his son-in-law, who in
turn passed them on to his son-in-law, thus only property received in marriage was bestowed through marriage.
A man greedy for honors endeavored to marry well and
often. It was not necessary in every case actually to
take the woman in order to acquire the honors. In
fact, if there were no daughter, a man might go through
the form of marriage with a man's foot in order to
perpetuate names and honors.

Not only was it necessary that a certain number of
inherited names or honors be acquired through marriage
in order that these socially elevating ceremonies may
be held; but the opportunities to acquire wealth had
to exist. Hunting and fishing grounds were the chief
possessions. Generally, also, slaves and dependent
relatives were required to assist the accumulation of
property. Also a great deal was added by skill and
application. Canoes were excellent forms of property

acquired through skill and labor alone. In early times, successful hunting resulted in the possession of furs and skins which were directly distributed; more recently, these were, of course, readily exchanged for woolen blankets which became the units of exchange.

A certain element of the population thus acquired fortune through birth and another through personal ability and activity. The inherited names were of little value unless the second element were added. Inherited names were only potential honors until assumed with lavish feasting and a distribution of wealth. But through personal achievement a man might greatly elevate his position during his life, and might bring about advancement for his descendants. Because of the social obligation to distribute this wealth, constant efforts had to be made to produce new assets. By including neighboring tribes in ceremonies of this sort it was possible to extend one's fame beyond the tribe. When a position had been acquired, it received constant public recognition, since a guest's name was proclaimed as he entered a house, and a seat assigned to him according to his rank.

Inherited Duties. There were many inherited public duties which brought the recipient no special renown. Among these, especially for the Kwakiutl, may be enumerated the public accounting of property. These public accountants were able to list the amount of property out on loan at any time; they were tally keepers, who counted and tallied blankets and other property when publicly transferred. There were also singers who improvised and taught songs to those initiated in certain societies. Among the Bella Coola one man inherited the duty of enforcing the taboos and regulations in regard to the river. Many specific duties

related to feasts and the taking or preparation of the
first fish or fruits of the season.

Exogamous Divisions. In addition to the grouping
according to tribe, sept, and village, some of the tribes
of this area had another type of social grouping, that
according to a rule of unilateral descent. Every member
of the tribe was by birth a member of one of these formal
divisions and by rule belonged to the same group as his
mother. This kind of social grouping is found in other
parts of America and elsewhere and is designated as a
clan or a sib system. As is nearly always the case,
these groups regulated marriage, that is, a man must
marry a woman from outside his own clan.

In order to understand the clan systems two essen-
tial points must be observed, first, that descent is
recorded either on the father's (paternal) or the
mother's (maternal) side; second, that all the members
of one's group are counted as relatives, and none of
them can be considered as a mate in marriage. On the
Northwest Coast this type of organization was known
among all of the tribes of the Tsimshian, Tlingit, and
Haida. Among the Tlingit and Haida and the Nass
River Tsimshian there were two such groups, while
among the other Tsimshian tribes there were four.
The Haida groups were called Eagle and Raven; those
of the Tlingit and Nass River Tsimshian, Raven and
Wolf; the Tsimshian proper and the Gitksan Tsimshian were grouped into Raven, Eagle, Wolf, and Bear.
Because a man and his wife were necessarily members of
different clans this divided the family as well as the
tribe. In addition to regulating marriage these groups
had certain religious, social, and political functions.

Among the Haida, until recently, the villages were
grouped according to location as, west coast, and east
coast, as well as south and north. Notwithstanding this

geographical grouping, and quite regardless of it, all the Haida were divided into two groups or clans, one called Ravens and the other Eagles. This division affected the whole tribe, because it runs also through every family. If the husband were a Raven his wife and children were Eagles; if the husband were an Eagle his wife and children were Ravens. Since, as has been stated above, such social grouping, is a well-recognized and widely distributed phenomenon, there is no reason to look for an origin of such groups in geographical distribution, or migration. The two essentials of such groups have been mentioned above; namely, descent in one line only, and an imputed relationship preventing marriage. In addition, there may be religious, social, and political distinctions as well. Among the Haida, the rank, names, ceremonial duties and properties, fishing rights, and house of a man had to remain in his own division. Since his children belonged to the opposite division, he chose for his heir, his sister's son; and in order that the sister's son might become familiar with the duties and properties he was to inherit, he lived with his uncle as soon as he was old enough to leave his mother. In case of violent quarrels between members of the two divisions a man's wife and sons adhered to their own clan and aligned themselves with his enemies, to whom they might even be expected to betray him.

The ceremonial connection of the Haida divisions was with burial and the accompanying rites. The body was prepared and buried by the father's family, members of the opposite division, which was recompensed by a potlatch. The division had no direct political functions since these pertain rather to the various families or septs. Since every sept belonged to either one of the divisions, and all the members of a sept were members of the same division, it was true that members of the same sept might not marry.

The Kwakiutl Bella Bella had four divisions in the north and five in the south; these were not marriage regulating, but merely local and social groups. They were equated, however, with the corresponding divisions of their northern neighbors and may be regarded as an attempt to imitate the social organization of the north.

In the south, the Salish counted descent and inherited, as we do, in both the father's and the mother's line. Usually a man sought a wife in some other village and brought her to his own village to live. A man's son was his usual heir, but a man also inherited honors and property from his mother's people, as well as from his father.

Among the Kwakiutl it is thought that a method originally similar to that of the Salish has been influenced from the north. The names and positions of the heads of various septs and families were inherited by the oldest son or daughter and their descendants. There were, however, many names carrying social and ceremonial positions, which were transmitted by a man through his son-in-law to his daughter's child. A child, other than the first born, may belong to his father's or his mother's sept (*numaym*) according to the parents' wishes. Whether a child was assigned to his father's or his mother's *numaym* usually depended upon the relative rank of the father and mother, and the privileges at their disposal. It was also a common practice, for a dying person to bestow his position by an expressed wish which was followed, if it were not too contrary to the established social customs. In certain of the noble Kwakiutl families an attempt was made to retain the privilege within the family by close intermarriage, such as between half brothers and sisters, or the marriage of a man with his younger brother's daughter.

The Bella Coola do not have such clearly marked divisions; and, in order to strengthen the family power and prestige, were much given to close intermarriage. Marriage between cousins or the children of cousins was not approved, but a union between the grand-children of cousins was regarded as ideal. It may be added that even among the northern tribes, where the divisions existed, the noble families intermarried, generation after generation, but always on the father's side.

PUBERTY

As among most primitive people the world over, the tribes of the Northwest Coast gave social and cere-monial recognition to the period of adolescence. At the time of puberty the girls of the Northwest Coast were, for a period, secluded, restricted as to their diet and movements, and observed special taboos. Even in the same tribe, there was considerable variation in detail as to these observances.

However, there was general agreement among the Northwest Coast tribes in placing the girl behind a screen; in requiring her to abstain from all food and drink for some days, and from certain foods for one or several years; and in guarding hunting, fishing, and gambling equipment, as well as fish and fish streams from her. Two kinds of reasons were assigned for these practices: First, that the girl herself would be influenced by conformity, or lack of conformity with these regula-tions. Whatever happened to her at this time would affect her throughout her life; second, that her actions would have an effect on other persons and on things. A hunter, meeting her, would lose his luck; salmon would fail to run if she saw them, or if she crossed the stream; should she look at a running dog it would be stopped by her glance. These reasons may be conceived of in part, as inventions to frighten the girl into obedience. Behind some of them, no doubt, lay the belief that the girl, during this time, was endowed with great supernatural or magical power. Among the Nootka the coming of age of a daughter was an occasion for giving a potlatch of special grandeur.

BURIAL CUSTOMS

Tree Burial. The Nootka and the southern Kwakiutl formerly resorted chiefly to tree burial. The bodies were folded and placed in large boxes which were carried into the tall timber and placed high up in a tree. Care was taken to select a tree rendered inaccessible because it leaned out over a chasm or over water; all the limbs below the body were also cut away so that climbing the tree thereafter would be difficult. The place chosen was some distance from the village, often on an island. Bodies were also placed in caves, provided suitable ones were available. Among the Nootka, the burial caves belonged to the more important families. The Kwakiutl viewed burial in the earth with considerable horror when contact with Europeans first brought the custom to their notice, but they have now adopted the practice.

Canoe Burial. The Salish tribes of Washington often used canoes as receptacles for the dead and their belongings. These were elevated on scaffolds or placed in trees beyond the reach of animals.

Cremation. The Tsimshian burned the dead except for the heart, which was removed and buried. With shamans, however, the internal organs were buried, and

Grave Post with Cavity in the Back of the Figure in which an Incinerated Body has been placed.   Wrangell, Tlingit.

Tree Burial near Alert Bay, B.C.   Kwakiutl.

the body placed in a grave house above ground. The
Haida and Tlingit also burned all but the shamans
whom they placed in grave houses in some isolated
place. The bones, after the cremation, were gathered
together and placed in elevated boxes or in mortuary
columns.

The intimate personal belongings of the deceased were
burned, or, in more recent times, placed near the grave.

Memorial Columns. It was the practice of all of the
tribes to erect a monument near the burial place of the
more prominent dead. Usually this consisted of a
wooden carving representing the principal crests of the
deceased. Recently similar carvings made in stone have
been substituted for wooden ones. Burial among
the northern tribes was always carried out by the
members of the clan or division of which the deceased
was not a member—that is by the members of
his father's division. Among the Tlingit and Haida,
those who buried a man were necessarily members
of his wife's clan. It was the rule among the
Kwakiutl to have people unrelated to them cut the
hair of the mourners. The performance of such duties
involved payment, which was accomplished in public
and with a feast; that is to say, it was a potlatch
occasion. Among the Tlingit it was the main occasion
for giving a potlatch and took place when the remains
were placed in their final resting place, and the mortuary
column was erected. Because the work was by the
opposite clan, they were the recipients of the distributed
property.

MARRIAGE

Selection of Mates. The choice of a mate was subject
to restrictions varying according to the tribal customs
and the social standing of the individuals concerned.

Memorial Columns, Anthony Island. Haida. Photograph by Doctor C. F. Newcombe.

101

Among all the tribes, it was almost indispensable that marriage should be between equals in rank. While this was the ideal, some accommodation to the supply and demand of mates was permitted; especially where the tribal population was small. In the south, among the Nootka and Salish, near relatives were avoided, whether on the father's or the mother's side. There was a tendency, moreover, among the Salish to marry outside the village. In the north, the Haida and Tlingit were divided into two exogamous matrilineal groups; therefore, and since a man always belonged to his mother's group, he must always select a mate from his father's group. The Tsimshian, being divided into four groups, were not compelled to marry into the father's clan.

The Kwakiutl of Vancouver Island and the neighboring mainland emphasized kinship in the father's sept and married into some other. There was, however, a counter tendency, especially in the families of higher rank, to intermarry in order to retain the crests and privileges within the sept.

The Bella Coola had neither matrilineal clans, nor exogamous regulations. On the other hand, intermarriage between certain families was customary in order to concentrate social possessions and social position, rather than suffer their dispersion through marriage with outsiders. Since rights and honors, in addition to those inherited, were mainly obtainable through marriage, a father eager to improve the position of his descendants will marry his daughter to several men in succession, even before she reaches puberty. The honors so accumulated passed on to his grandchildren, regardless of which particular man was their parent. Marriage between cousins or children of cousins was not allowed, but the most favored marriage was be-

tween grandchildren of cousins. Intermarriage between certain related families continued for generations.

While, as stated above, the northern tribes always
avoided the mother's group there was no such regulation in regard to the father's relatives. The conventional marriage for a Tsimshian youth was with his
mother's younger brother's daughter. The rule that
only those equal in rank should mate, greatly reduced
the choice of the few families of high station so that
constant intermarriage on the father's side became
necessary. It was formerly the custom for the head
chiefs of two of the more important Tsimshian tribes
to marry each other's sister, generation after generation. So complicated were the various social conditions
among the Tlingit, that the choice of a mate for a
member of the higher aristocracy, was sometimes reduced to two or three individuals.

Equality in age was not given much consideration.
Among the northern tribes, where the sister's scn succeeded his uncle, inheriting property and privileges
from him, he was expected to marry his uncle's widow.
When he became older, however, there was an opportunity to secure a bride much younger than himself.
Such inequalities of age were regarded with favor.

Marriage Customs. There was considerable uni-
formity throughout the area in the method of carrying
out marriages. Everywhere it was the custom for a
family to reside in the village of the husband. The
general custom seemed to have been for the bridegroom's relatives to approach the bride's family
formally, with presents or promises of presents. A
certain degree of hesitation was ordinarily shown by the
bride's family, which took the form, as it did with the
Salish in the south, of keeping the bridegroom waiting
and fasting for some days. The Nootka and Kwakiutl

had certain ordeals peculiar to each particular family, which had to be passed successfully by the groom, or by his representatives. One such ordeal was to compel the bridegroom to pass by a very hot fire. There was often also some bickering over the value of the presents offered; not of a mercenary character, but to emphasize the high standing of the parties concerned. The acceptance of the presents by the bride's family was followed by return gifts of equal or greater value. By the Salish these were delivered within a few days to the village of the bridegroom where the bride was taken to reside.

Among the Kwakiutl, the bride's father announced, at the time of the wedding, that he would give his son-in-law certain property and honors. These were usually not delivered until a child was born to the couple, and often, not until the child was old enough to be initiated into the ceremonies. The amount given by the bride's father was sometimes five times that received from the bridegroom, but this varied according to the number and sex of the children. The Kwakiutl considered that this payment dissolved the marriage. The wife, if she were the first one, ordinarily continued to live with her husband, but with a greater degree of independence since she was free to return to her home if she wished. If her husband were ambitious for honors and able to pay for them, he made presents again to his father-in-law, renewing his marriage. In due time he received in return more than he had given in property, as well as additional names and honors. In all these cases the transfer of property took place at a public gathering where the witnesses were feasted. Since the property thus received was distributed to the husband's sept within a day or two, the son-in-law benefitted, not in property, but only in the new and higher honors which he had received. However, in all ordinary cases, he transferred these to his son, or his daughter's husband, in the same manner as he himself had received them.

The Haida mother often made an engagement for her son or daughter while they were still quite young and ensured its validity by a present of blankets. The family of the boy took the initiative among the Masset and the family of the girl among the Skidegate. When the ceremony occurred, the speeches made by the boy's relatives praised the girl and her family, while her own spokesmen belittled her and her abilities. This procedure was the reverse of that among the Nootka, where each party bestowed praises on his own family.

GAMES

The Northwest Coast people were quite addicted to gambling. The most popular game was the well-known and widely distributed one of guessing by the expression of the opponent's face where a marked stick was concealed. The objects necessary were a number of sets of sticks about three-eighths of an inch in diameter and five inches long. The sticks of the same set were painted with the same pattern except the "ace" which was unmarked. Each set had a bag and a larger one held the various sets of the owner. The sets of sticks were laid out on a piece of skin, the playing was on a mat, the sticks were displayed on a second piece of hide while the guess was made. The opponents sat facing each other. The first player selected one of his sets of sticks, wrapped them in cedarbark, and divided them into two bundles which he placed before himself. His opponent then attempted to guess, by a study of the player's expression, in which bundle the "ace" was concealed. If he guessed correctly, he took the play, but if not, the former player continued. When one side attained a count of seven, four bundles were made instead of two; the player won the final point only if the guesser missed it after three trials. Such odds greatly prolonged the game. This game varied as to the objects used, but the main point, that of guessing from the opponent's expression and reactions was the same.

There were, in addition, dice games, shooting at a mark, a form of quoits, shinney, wrestling, and numerous other games. The stones used in the latter game were frequently found near the village sites. The Northwest Coast people, in common with those all over the world, had string figures or cat's cradles.

WARFARE

While many of the winter villages were located with a view to comfortable living rather than defense, certain other village sites were chosen with an evident desire for security from attack. Ordinarily, a point of land was occupied so that the only approach was by a narrow passageway which could be cut off by means of ditches and stockades. In most instances these forts could be reduced by a few days' siege, for the Indians were not accustomed to long continued and tenacious fighting.

Two sorts of armor were used. One kind was made of a double thickness of heavy skin, worn like a shirt. Some of these shirts were long, reaching nearly to the knees, while others reached only to the hips. They were generally sleeveless, but some examples have a sleeve for the left arm, the right arm being free for use. One of Captain Cook's men amazed the Nootka by shooting a musket ball through one of these skin shirts folded six times. The second type of armor was composed of flat or round sticks, placed vertically side by side and held securely by horizontal stout twined cord lacings. It was worn like a waistcoat, tied in place with leather strings at the right side.

In addition, there were protective wooden pieces for the neck and face, reaching up under the eyes, and above these, a helmet was worn. Such armor provided very excellent protection against clubs, lances, and arrows.

For offense, bows and arrows were sometimes employed. Short spears were also used, both for thrusting and throwing. The Tlingit had two-edged knives, with a carved wood or bone handle, or two-edged and pointed at either end with a hand grip considerably to one side of the middle. Formerly, these knives were made of bone and probably also of native copper. They were customarily worn either suspended from the neck, or thrust into the belt. Clubs were also employed; some were of the bones of whales, and others of wood, long and heavy enough to crush a skull. Most curious of all were the pickax-like weapons, mentioned by Captain Cook, a Tlingit example of which is in the Museum collections. Mention may also be made of a peculiarly shaped stone club generally referred to as a slave killer.

The two chief occasions for fighting were: revenge, and the securing of slaves. The feeling for a just balance, a life for a life, or an injury for an injury, was strongly developed and was active between families, villages, and larger groups. In several respects the Indians' views of such matters were quite unlike our own. In recent times, we have come to feel that retaliation for death or injury should fall upon the guilty individuals, but the Indians were as well satisfied if they took revenge on any member of the same group, or a person living in the same region. An example of this may be seen in a recorded account of the Kwakiutl. A canoe with its passengers, one of whom was a chief, failed to return from Victoria. Evidence pointed to indulgences in liquor and the resulting inability to navigate the boat properly. A war party went to the vicinity of Victoria and while they slept killed the first group of Indians found in that region. The motive

Double-Edged and Double-Bladed Knife, made of Bone of Whale. Tlingit.

Warclub made of Whale's Rib. Tlingit.

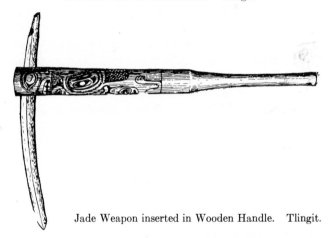

Jade Weapon inserted in Wooden Handle. Tlingit.

was rather clearly shown to be the satisfaction afforded the living relatives and some assumed benefits thought to accrue to the souls of those who have met a violent death.

As might be expected, where rank was so important as on the Pacific Coast, a life for a life was not always satisfactory. When a man had been killed in a village, the Tlingit were said to have conferred as to his worth and then to have chosen as the object of their retaliation a man of equal value in the offending group. He was publicly called upon to come forth and be killed. The man actually guilty, being of too little worth to satisfy justice, escaped, or settled matters with the family of the man slain in his stead.

From the accounts available it appears that the usual method of waging war was as follows: The proposal for a war expedition was made in a public assembly by some man of influence. It was then determined whether other groups should be invited to coöperate with them, and a time was set for the expedition to leave. The warriors and their wives underwent purification; in the south, at least, this consisted of frequent bathing followed by scrubbing with boughs, fasting, and continence. The canoes were raised, scorched, and freshly rubbed on the outside. Certain religious and magical acts were performed to secure good luck. The wives were required to follow established rules of conduct in order to bring good fortune to the party. Travel was always by canoe; the crews were organized; with each was a man provided with kindlings for setting fire to houses, one with ropes for securing slaves, and guards to watch the canoes. Due care was exercised that information should not reach the enemy. The arrival was timed for the evening and the attack for the morning, at about dawn, that the victims might be caught asleep. At dusk a small scouting canoe was sent out. The exact number and position of the houses was noted and the attack planned accordingly, each canoe crew being assigned to a definite house. If revenge were the motive, men and women would be killed, but if the expedition were to secure slaves unnecessary slaughter, especially of women, was avoided.

CHAPTER IV

RELIGION AND CEREMONIAL LIFE

In dealing with so difficult a subject as religion it is well to take up various aspects in detail. One profitable division of the subject is into the beliefs concerning the universe on one hand, and on the other, the specific acts and general conduct which seem to have religious motives. On analysis the elaborate ceremonies of the Northwest Coast, which at first might be assumed to be mainly religious in character, prove to be largely dramatic, with the social and artistic features fully as prominent as the religious aspects.

Religious Beliefs. Religious beliefs were concerned with the past, the present, and the future. Beliefs regarding the past and the origin of the world were largely speculative and were generally formulated in myths which did not necessarily have much connection with human conduct. Those dealing with the future were also speculative and related particularly to the persistence of personality after death. The concept of the supernatural world was, however, of the greatest importance, since it very greatly influenced daily life.

Supreme Being. There is no evidence that a belief in a supreme being was general, but among the Haida and the Bella Coola, it appears that such a definite conception did exist.

Haida Deities. The Haida refer to the supreme being as the Power of the Shining Heavens. They believed that human beings had no direct personal relations with this being, who is conceived of as the source from which all the other minor supernatural beings derived their power. It was with these secondary deities that man dealt. There were houses believed to be suspended from the sky, in one of which dwelt Wigit who kept account of all human beings, and, who when a baby was about to be born, reached behind himself and pulled out a stick, the length of which regulated the duration of the child's life.

Of the supernatural beings on the earth, the Creek-women were of great importance. Each stream was believed to have a female divinity whose abode was at the source of the river. She controlled the stream and all the fish in it. Another Creek-woman, Djilagons by name, was also an important mythological character. Underneath the Queen Charlotte Islands which constitute the Haida world stood "the sacred one standing and moving." His infrequent movements produced the earthquakes. Thunderbird was responsible for lightning and thunder.

In addition to these beings which from our point of view are purely imaginary, the Haida considered that practically all fish, birds, and land and sea mammals were similar to human beings, but possessed of varying degrees of supernatural power. All of them were capable of taking human form; or better, they possessed a human form, and assumed their other forms when consorting with men. Of all living things, the killer-whales were the greatest. They were believed to live in villages under the sea, usually near some point of land. These under-sea villages were definitely located and named. The body of the killer-whale was nothing but the canoe in which he was accustomed to travel. There were also salmon people, herring people, and on land, grizzly bear people, land-otter people, etc. It was not always clear whether the supernatural land-otter people, for instance, were or were not distinct from the animal. Probably there was much confusion in the native mind on this subject. It is important, however, to keep in mind that the Indian attitude toward animals was extremely different from our own. In their mythology are frequent references to a time when the animals were men, gifted with the power of speech and other human attributes. The people of the Northwest Coast believed that animals have souls which are immortal and that they are re-born after death. They are considered practically the equals of man in general intelligence, and to surpass him in the particulars for which the animal in question is especially noted.

Among the Haida, these animals were also divided into two sections: Ravens and Eagles corresponding to their two social groups. The killer-whales are differently marked so they can be distinguished; the Eagles have a white patch at the base of the dorsal fin. Many of the taboos and customs observed in hunting and fishing were adjustments to bring about social harmony between men and the "other peoples" used for food. One needs to realize that these were not, to the Indian's way of thinking, mythological beings, but real beings upon whose good will they were dependent.

Bella Coola Deities. The Bella Coola concept of the supernatural was somewhat similar, being rather more definitely systematized. There are five worlds, one above the other, ours being the middle one. On the highest, toward the east was the house of a woman, all powerful, but disinterested in worldly affairs. On the second world, the one directly above us, was the House of Myths, the home of the principal deities. As far as the actual control of the world is concerned, the most important may be considered the supreme being. He was appealed to in prayer by men. He was thought of often as traveling in the sun, but he was by no means inseparable from it. He made a soul for each of those about to be born; one of the minor gods fashioned its face; and a goddess rocked it, and sent it below to be born. In a like manner, all the animals were made and sent below for birth. In the House of Myths also lived the mother of the flowers, who each spring gave birth to the plants in the order in which they appeared on earth. Deaths as well as births were there determined. Minor deities were charged with the control of the secret ceremonials which were held upon the earth in the winter.

Gods of the Kwakiutl. The Kwakiutl, like the Bella Coola, believed that the supernatural ones lived in houses, but unlike the Bella Coola, the Kwakiutl made the mysterious, heavily forested inland region, rather than the upper world, the home of these supernatural beings. Most frequently mentioned was the house in the north where lived the cannibal spirit who gave the Kwakiutl their most prized ceremony, and who was still believed to initiate all the candidates received into the Cannibal Society. Of more general religious significance was another house from which a different type of winter ceremony was derived. Incidentally, it appears that in this house the souls of all the plants, and perhaps also the smaller animals dwell. Since one of the performances held in this house was that of giving birth, it was probably believed that from this house all generation of men, animals, and plants, took place. In addition to these two houses somewhere on land there was one under the sea belonging to the killer-whales who are the greatest hunters of sea life. The Kwakiutl like the Haida considered all animals as potentially human-like and capable of assuming the appearance of men. The mountain goats, like the killer-whales, had a house in which they lived, as men do. Even the one domesticated animal, the dog, might assume a human form.

It is clear that the dominating religious concept was that bodies of men, animals, and plants, were the houses, canoes, or shells in which souls dwelt and that these souls had a great range of action outside of the habitations in which they were ordinarily found. The following Tsimshian myth will illustrate the attitude of the people toward the "salmon people."

A young prince was scolded by his mother for taking a certain dry salmon to give to his hungry slave. The prince was grieved and went down near the river. A canoe came, he entered, and was taken far out to sea. He arrived at a village where the carvings on the houses indicated that they belonged to Spring Salmon. The chief had been ill because the prince's mother had kept the dry salmon for two years and that particular salmon was his body. The slave's eating it had in some measure aided his recovery and, out of gratitude, he had sent for the prince. Whenever the prince was hungry he was instructed to club one of the children playing outside. The child immediately became a spring salmon. The prince was charged to put in the fire all the bones left after his meal. If this were done to the bones of the salmon, they would come to life again in their own country. Dry salmon must not be kept beyond the next season, for otherwise they are not released by being eaten and by the burning of their bones. When once the prince overlooked an eye, a child complained that one of his eyes hurt. As soon as the prince found the missing eye and burned it, the child's eye was well again.

In spring the salmon chief, now fully recovered, sent scouts to the Skeena and Nass rivers to see if the cottonwood leaves were floating on the river. As soon as they were found, a journey was made to all the villages of the salmon people, and they were notified. Each variety of salmon had its own village from which the canoes set out in proper succession to go to the rivers where they appeared to the fishermen in their fish form. The chief of the spring salmon went to the shaman's net. After his names had been called over him he was cut open and was used in a feast from which all who were ceremonially unclean were excluded. All his bones were put in the fire and those who had eaten took a drink of fresh water. The prince was found in this chief salmon's stomach and rapidly grew to his former size. He instructed the people as to the things which must be observed in regard to salmon and finally returned to live with the salmon people.

Such concepts of an animal world, closely interrelated with the world of human beings, furnish much of the religious life and emotional atmosphere of the Northwest Coast.

Religious Practices

Ceremonial Purity. In response to the religious ideas outlined in the last section, certain efforts were made to keep on good terms with the supernatural beings. Many rituals were performed in order to achieve ceremonial cleanliness. The supernatural beings were supposed to be very sensitive to odors. In part, this may be an entirely natural and practical observation in so far as it concerns game animals. Cleanliness was achieved by ritualistic bathing. For certain ceremonial occasions the baths were in the sea, but the most beneficial were in freshwater lakes. After the bath, the body was scrubbed with hemlock branches, often until the blood ran. Such baths were taken night and morning for four days or in four different lakes. A man undertaking ceremonial duties was obliged to practise continence for days and sometimes weeks in advance. Women, unless well past middle age, were always of doubtful cleanliness, and were sometimes excluded from ceremonies as a matter of precaution. Abstention from food and water was believed to contribute greatly to an acceptable condition and for the same purpose the stomach was emptied by emetics.

While these efforts to secure personal purity were sometimes made so that game, viewed as supernatural, would not be offended and driven away, they also rendered the body an acceptable abode for any spirit that might wish to possess it. Once a spirit looking through a smoke-hole saw a Tlingit youth nearly dead from his fasts, but so clean as to be transparent like glass. In the Plains region, and elsewhere, similar means were pursued, but the Plains people considered that the supernatural ones pitied the man's suffering, a concept not common on the Northwest Coast.

Offerings. Food offerings, especially fat, were made. For water beings, the offerings were dropped into the sea, but for most other beings the gifts were placed in the fire. These offerings were not of any considerable bulk or value and do not seem to have been made with an idea of purchasing favors or goodwill. They were, rather, forms of social politeness.

Taboos. Many taboos had to be observed for fear of evil results. Naturally, many of these were concerned with salmon and fishing. Among the Tsimshian only mussel shells could be used for cutting salmon and among all the tribes metals were at first thought to be offensive. Mackenzie and other early travelers found it difficult to buy fresh salmon, the Indians fearing the fish would be cut with metal knives and cooked in metal dishes since it was believed that breaking of a taboo would "shame" the salmon and they would cease to run up the rivers.

The first salmon taken each year received special treatment. The Bella Coola placed it on a mat with its head on a pillow and offered it a piece of cedarbark. Afterward, eagle down was strewn over it and it was carried to the house and roasted. The Kwakiutl prayed to the first salmon caught each year and ate them immediately in a feast to which the men of the sept were invited.

The Nootka were accustomed to bring a bear which had been killed into the house, place it in a sitting position, put a hat on it, and sprinkle it with eagle down. The bear was offered food and invited to eat. The Tlingit also carried the grizzly bear's head into the house and decorated it with paint and eagle down.

Shamanism

Among all primitive peoples, certain individuals, called shamans by ethnologists, are supposed to have unusual and supernatural powers. Among the tribes of the Northwest Coast there were both men and women shamans. Their extraordinary powers were believed by the Indians to come from supernatural beings who, at particular times, possessed the shaman and spoke through him. Among the Haida and Tlingit a powerful shaman had a considerable number of spirit helpers for each of which there was a special mask. When the influence of a particular being was felt, his mask was worn and the shaman spoke the language of that spirit. Among the northern tribes, the calling of the shaman was usually inherited, his power passing later to his nephew. The dying man informed his heir as to the spirits which would inspire him and gave him the necessary instructions. In after years the novice increased his powers by obtaining additional spiritual assistants. The uninitiated, at least, believed that in all cases the shaman acquired his power through a visitation or seizure by a supernatural being. The shaman's soul journeyed with that of the supernatural being and visited the abode of his helper and received magical power and gifts. In the meantime, the body of the shaman lay in a trance in his own house. In some instances, the spirits sought the man and he thus became a shaman against his will.

In the treatment of the sick, a shaman, after dancing with his rattle was supposed to see the cause of the disorder, usually some natural or supernatural object lodged in the body which became visible to him. It may be that the patient had passed behind a shaman who had swallowed his soul. In that case the dancing

shaman was presumably able to see the sick man's soul
in the other shaman's stomach. The soul of the patient
may have left his body and gone to the graveyard or
into the woods. The actual curing required that the
foreign object be removed from the body, or that the

Model representing
a Shaman with Raven
Symbols. Haida.

soul be restored, if it had wan-
dered away. In the first case,
sucking was resorted to and the
object was produced from the
shaman's mouth. In the second,
the shaman went to the place
where the strayed soul had been
seen by him and caught it between
his palms. He displayed it and
placed it on the patient's head.

Shamans served the commu-
nity not only in the curing of the
sick but some of them were able
to foretell events and to see what
was happening in distant parts.
Every war party included a
shaman who through his supernatural knowledge warned of
danger and pointed out favorable
times and places for attacks. The
shaman, by catching or destroying the souls of the enemy, made
the killing of their bodies an easy

matter. A powerful shaman would be able to tell where
a stranded whale was to be found, or to cause their
stranding and was also able to influence the run of fish.

His costume was peculiar; his hair was never cut nor
dressed in any way. Suspended from his neck he wore a
bone head-scratcher and a tube through which he blew
on his patients. He also wore a long bone through the

septum of his nose. On various occasions, he displayed his power particularly by walking through fire; often he entered into contests with rival shamans when their respective spirit helpers engaged in combat.

Among the northern tribes, when a shaman died, he was buried, not cremated, and supernatural power remained in the vicinity of his grave house which was at a

Model of a Shaman's Grave Box. Haida.

distance from the village. His soul was said to go to a special abode, usually in the sky. Among the Tlingit, shamans rivaled the chiefs in the power exercised over the people.

Winter Ceremonies

Throughout the Northwest Coast there were secret societies which gave dramatizations of myths during the winter. To the uninitiated, the actors appeared to be possessed by supernatural beings and to perform miracles. From their viewpoint, at least, these ceremonies were chiefly religious. Those who were engaged in the performances prepared the properties, rehearsed with care, and endeavored to act so realistically as to deceive their audiences. These occasions were dramatic, or theatrical, However, since the presentations were dramatizations of the acts of supernatural mythical beings, or manifestations of present-day supernatural power, the religious element may be considered as predominating.

These winter ceremonies were in their main features common over the entire area. They were begun at a rather definite moment when supernatural beings and powers were thought to arrive and remain in the villages. The moment of their arrival was announced by the sound of whistles which, in theory at least, the uninitiated thought was made by the spirits of the winter ceremony. These whistles were heard during the ceremony whenever those possessed of some supernatural spirit were present or were performing. Since feasting and distribution of property were constantly taking place at this time of the year, the social features were especially pronounced. The events were planned and controlled by the nobility since only this class was able to provide the necessary food and gifts.

The ceremonial features were built up around the belief that one or more persons, usually young, were taken to the homes of the supernatural beings who gave them songs and instruction, and possessed them, causing them to act in an insane manner. When they reappeared they had to be captured and restored to a normal condition. They were, however, subject to seizure in the future whenever the ceremony was held for others, or when any event suggested their supernatural experiences to them.

Kwakiutl Ceremonies. A description of one of the ceremonies of a Kwakiutl secret society will give some idea
of the nature of these rituals. The annual ceremony
was initiated by an announcement made by some man
that he wished his son to assume membership in the
society to which he held a right. This privilege of
membership was usually secured through marriage. A
man's father-in-law at the time of the marriage promised
to give him his place in a secret society. This membership, however, was generally held in trust for the
children of the newly married couple. When a son was
of proper age to assume his membership his father asked
that the promise be fulfilled. At this time also the
father-in-law returned to his son-in-law the payment
made at the time of the marriage, with additional
property, often four or five times the value he received
for his daughter. The chiefs consulted to make sure
that the man and his relatives had sufficient wealth to
carry through the ceremony properly. The whole
tribe was convened and notice given of the prospective
ceremony. The winter dance pole was brought in
and the man and his father-in-law announced the
amount of property to be transferred. The people were
directed to purify themselves during the succeeding
four days by bathing in the sea in the early morning.
After the bath, they rubbed themselves with hemlock
branches. All relations between the sexes must cease
because the spirits of the winter ceremonies were about
to come to the village and human odors are offensive to
them. As the assembly dispersed, the young man who
was about to take his place in the society disappeared
with a characteristic cry. The people were reminded
that he had been taken by the cannibal spirit to his
home in the north where he would be initiated by the
supernatural people living there. He was expected

back at the end of four days at which time the people were requested to reassemble.

The house of the winter ceremonies was cleared out and prepared for the celebrations. After four days had passed, the people were summoned to this house by special messengers. It will be remembered that when the northwestern people came to a feast or formal assembly they were always seated according to rank by clans, families, septs, tribes, etc. During the winter ceremony, however, they were grouped according to the societies to which they belonged. These societies fell into two main divisions, the more important called the seal society was composed of all the dancing or drama-acting bodies. The various societies forming the seals are graded in importance, at their head being the *hamatsa* or cannibal society. The less important division also consisted of graded societies bearing animal names in which the people were grouped according to sex and age. Between these two groups existed much rivalry and assumed enmity. Not only were the people differently grouped during the winter ceremony, but each individual had a special name by which he had to be called during this period. This was no doubt, a recognition of what was believed to be a changed or different personality. The various societies arrived at the house in groups and were assigned seats together. The seal society came in last and was seated at the rear of the house with the cannibal society in the place of highest honor. The master of ceremonies circled the fire singing and swinging his rattle. The assembled people sang, each individual singing his own secret song.

Other men took this opportunity to have children initiated so that the ceremony was repeated as many times as there were novices.

A Youth showing the Hemlock Decoration of a Novice.
Kwakiutl.

There were feasts at night and, during the next three days, much singing and dancing. Meantime, the father-in-law turned over the promised property to his son-in-law, the father of the boy who was absent with the supernatural ones being initiated by them. The third evening those who had previously been initiated were called to an assembling place in the woods where they were taught new songs by the singing masters who composed them. The novice and his assistant, a kins-woman, were nearby in the woods, listening, so that they would be able to dance to the songs when the ceremony was held.

The people of the village were formally called to the assembly house soon after dark. The messengers entered each house in the village and called the names of the inmates in the order of their society rank. When they had assembled, individuals came in, one after the other and performed one of the dances which they possessed. At the door were heralds who announced the dancers. There was much fun and good-natured raillery. Occasionally, messengers were sent out to see if the novice were returning. Toward morning the ghost dancer appeared and his song was sung. The older members of the *hamatsa* society suddenly entered the house from both ends and through the roof. They cried "Hap hap" and danced around the fire four times in a squatting position. The novice was supposed to be attracted by their cries. He was heard on the roof, and after running around four times, he pushed a roof plank aside three times, and the fourth time, jumped down. While some tried to catch him he ran around the fire four times and disappeared through a secret door in the rear of the house, leaving behind him the hemlock branches which were his clothing. He

Fool Dancers of the Winter Ceremony.   Kwakiutl.

Cannibal Society of Winter Ceremony.   Kwakiutl.

entered and disappeared three times and then the assembly was dismissed.

After a short rest the people were assembled on the beach, where joining hands, they formed a square, and tried to surround the novice who appeared, then disappeared, only to appear suddenly again at a distant and unexpected place. The fourth time he was caught through the device of placing a naked man in front of him; the novice rushed up to him and bit his arm. The kinswoman helper who had been in the woods with him during the four days now appeared and danced into the house backward to lure the novice in. After much delay, he entered and rushed about, biting the arms of different people. He repeatedly fled to a room in the rear of the house which had been provided for him. After much singing and dancing he was restored to his senses.

Later, in private, a few of the leaders purified the newly initiated man and his female attendant. The property received from his father-in-law by the man giving the ceremony was publicly distributed. Payment had to be made to all persons bitten by the "cannibal." Incidentally, there were minor initiations and much supplementary feasting.

Ordinarily, there were initiations, similar to the one outlined above, given by other groups resident in the village or temporarily there as guests. Each had its own ceremony, differing from the others in minor details. When given together there was much rivalry to see which group could give the most spectacular and mystifying performance.

In theory, the cannibal novice, while absent, had become accustomed to eating corpses. It is said that formerly his woman attendant enticed him into the assembly house by holding in front of him a corpse secured from the nearby village burial place. The candidate was said to have eaten the dried skin from the body and to have been joined in his feasting by the older members of the society. Often there would be contests to see which group had a cannibal society member who could outdo the others in corpse-eating. There are also accounts of slaves being killed to supply fresh food for the cannibals. The biting and pretended eating of dogs caught up alive was the more common indication of frenzy shown by the northern tribes.

Magical Performances. During the ceremonies at night in the assembly house there were many exhibitions of sleight-of-hand. A common trick was for a woman who had great supernatural power to invite someone to run her through with a spear or to cut off her head. A shaman restored her and took her underground in spite of all attempts to hold her. During one such exhibition a woman was struck by a paddle which seemed to cleave her shoulder well down to her breast. Blood was seen to flow in abundance. These performances were, of course, arranged in advance and executed with the aid of confederates. The head displayed as severed was realistically carved of wood. The blood which flowed was enclosed in a bladder and was released by the blow. The spear supposed to be thrust through the body telescoped; and, by means of a string attached to the skin, it could be made to appear that the point of the spear raised the skin on the opposite side of the body. The corpse eating described above, no doubt, belonged also with these sleight-of-hand performances. Under the circumstances it is difficult to know how much of religious attitude and belief there was on the part of the initiated who planned and carried out the winter ceremonies. It is probable that they did believe that the candidate was in some degree possessed by the cannibal spirit and that those who appeared in masks were temporarily acting as substitutes for the supernatural beings themselves. The deliberate deceptions were to impress the uninitiated by greatly exaggerating the display of supernatural power which was sincerely believed to exist in less evident forms.

Supernatural Visitors. The chief religious significance of these ceremonies may be the belief that during this period of the winter ceremony the invisible supernatural beings, at other times remote, were, for the time being, among men and in close social contact with them. This belief was clearly indicated for the Bella Coola who divided their year into two parts. During nine months the canoe of the salmon was in the Bella Coola country. As it departed, another canoe bringing the winter ceremony arrived, and remained four months. When it departed, the salmon canoe returned. The Bella Coola winter ceremony, in a general way, was similar to that of the Kwakiutl. It was believed by them to have been derived from their neighbors, the Bella Bella.

Haida Ceremonies. The Haida secret ceremonies were always combined with potlatches. Such affairs were only attempted after the salmon season, for then the people were assembled in the winter villages, had sufficient leisure, and an abundance of food for the feasts. The Haida myths placed the supernatural houses where the initiation of the first novice took place under the sea. These locations were in the Tsimshian waters and, therefore, they claimed that the ceremonies were Tsimshian in origin. There were several varieties of societies, fire throwers, dog eaters, etc., but, in the main, the performances were similar to those described for the Kwakiutl. The mysterious whistles were used and called spirits; arms were bitten; the novice was killed and restored to life. The right to be initiated was inherited or bestowed by one who had inherited it. Sleight-of-hand and dramatic performances were also provided.

Tlingit Ceremonies. The Tlingit had such ceremonies only when a potlatch was held after the death of a prominent man, when his remains were entombed and the memorial erected. The subdivisions of the opposite clan give the performances with much rivalry, often involving serious conflicts. Each sept owned a wand or standard which, if set up between groups about to fight, immediately inhibited the conflict.

POTLATCH

The word "potlatch" comes from the Chinook jargon and originally meant "to give." In its common use among the white people and the natives on the Northwest Coast it has taken on a very general meaning and applied to any Indian festival at which there is feasting, or, in connection with which property is given away. Because of this loose and general meaning there necessarily exists a good deal of confusion as to what is meant by the term. From the Indian's viewpoint many different things are meant when he uses the Chinook word in speaking to white people, for it is the only word intelligible to them by means of which he can refer to a considerable number of ceremonies or festivals each having its own Indian name.

In the potlatch there are perhaps two main principles involved: first that all events of social or political interest must be publicly witnessed; and second that those who perform personal or social service must be publicly recompensed. A third more general social law is that all guests on all occasions must be fed. If we may judge from the more widely distributed aspects of the ceremonies of the various tribes along the coast, potlatches were primarily the accompaniment of certain crises in the life of an individual.

A child under a year old was not called by name but was referred to by the place of its birth. When it was a year old a name was given it; and presents of a mat or paddle were made to its relatives. At ten or twelve a boy received another name and there was a greater distribution of property. The girls reached maturity at a somewhat more advanced age, at which time among the Nootka a very important feast with a lavish distribution of property took place. At a less definite age the boy was initiated into the secret society to which he had an inherited or an acquired claim. This was also an event of great importance among the southern tribes. As has been described above, betrothal and marriage were also potlatch occasions. Of still greater importance was the ceremony at which the father-in-law made return gifts, which usually took place some years after the marriage.

Among the northern tribes, Haida, Tlingit, and Tsimshian, the main potlatch occasion occurred after the death of an important person when the final burial rites were held, the remains entombed, and a memorial to the dead erected. The burial duties devolved upon the family of the father of the deceased, connected of course with the opposite, or at least a different clan. At the time of the ceremony those who attended to the burial were recompensed. At this time, moreover, there were exhibitions of dancing by the other members of the clan of the deceased and a distribution of property to them also.

The building of a house required the hiring of various individuals who secured the timbers and assisted in putting them in place and in the ornamentation of the house with carvings and paintings. The potlatch has often been confused with the winter ceremonies which were the occasions for initiations into the secret societies mentioned above.

One prominent feature of all the events enumerated above was the assumption of a new name by the giver of the feast. This always meant an advance in standing and rank and was perhaps the strongest motive behind the whole potlatch system.

Since all these occasions required the dispensing of hospitality, considerable supplies of food were necessary and were accumulated by unusual activities in fishing and food gathering on the part of the man and his family, or, in recent years, by the purchase of provisions from traders with money received as wages. The second requisite was a supply of presents for distribution. These formerly consisted of slaves, canoes, and clothing, especially skins. More recently, the gray Hudson Bay blankets superseded nearly all other forms of property. These blankets could, of course, also be accumulated through purchase from the traders as a result of thrift. Such blankets when given away were not ordinarily used as apparel, but were hoarded as a sort of currency. Although an individual was the principal figure in a potlatch, it was not entirely a personal matter. His family and relatives were also interested and bound by tradition to assist in making it a success. They were drawn upon for blankets which might be returned to them later.

When property was publicly distributed it fell into two categories, as payment for services rendered, or as compensation for injuries. This was a limited transaction and the obligation was canceled. The greater amount of property was given to invited guests, to each according to his rank. Such gifts could be declined and became binding obligations upon the recipient and his heirs, so that when he in turn gave a potlatch, he had to re-pay more than an equivalent to this man, or his heirs. In this second case, giving was really profitable lending. Among the Kwakiutl such forced lending was not confined to public occasions. If a man were planning to give a potlatch, he lent his stock of blankets some months before the event and collected them again with considerable interest.

The main purpose of the potlatch may be assumed to have been the impression made on the public mind. It was this which elevated the man and his family in the public estimation. The more widely the invitations were sent out, the more spectacular the display of property, and the more lavish the feasting, the greater and deeper was the emotional result and the longer did it endure. To increase this effect the property was publicly displayed on the beach. As a permanent record, posts were erected at either end of the long piles of blankets. Often too, in more recent years, inscriptions were placed over the man's door and added to his grave monument so that the event would not be forgotten.

THE FUTURE WORLD

The most characteristic belief among the tribes of the Northwest Coast in regard to the fate of souls after death was that it depended upon the kind of death by which they were freed. The larger number, those who died of old age or disease, went toward the west and had to cross water barriers, usually rivers. There was some disagreement whether the world of dead was on the same level as this or below it. Life in that world was similar to this, but much less agreeable. To some extent the souls depended on their surviving relatives for food and clothing. The latter was chiefly supplied at the time of the funeral, but food was sent frequently by placing it in the fire. Singing after a death was an advantage to the traveling soul for it illuminated the trail, and, according to the Haida, permitted the soul to enter its new abode with its head up. Those who died by drowning went to the underwater deities, the killer-whales. Offerings for them were put in fires near the seashore or thrown into the ocean. The souls of those killed in warfare went to a world above, by no means a paradise, but a fairly endurable place. Those who died unavenged had difficulty in climbing up.

Shaman's souls also went to a special place—according to the Haida, an island. Certain of the shaman's powers continued an association with the body which, it will be remembered, was given a different sort of burial from that accorded an ordinary person.

A second death was believed to be possible so that the soul passed from the first place of the dead to another, either below the first or farther to the west. Some of the souls, perhaps the majority, were reborn, usually in the same family to which they belonged in the first instance.

The Bella Coola believed that at death three separate entities survived. One of these went above to the House of Myths, a second to the world of the dead, the next below this world, and a third part manifested itself here in the hooting of the owl.

Mythology and Folklore

The myths of a people are generally assumed to be a formulation of their beliefs in the supernatural origins of the world and of mankind and his social institutions, that is, they are a system of belief which explains the world as it is. In so far as they treat of the supernatural they may be viewed as religious in character. But in addition to accounts of the creation of the world, of a

flood, and other momentous events, there are usually
found many trivial and ludicrous narratives and incidents. It is evident that the creative imagination of
mankind has been at work and the gods and heroes are
made to furnish amusement by their adventures and
pranks. We are dealing then, to a certain extent, with
unwritten literature rather than with religion. In North
American mythology there are a number of characters
who are at the same time gods and tricksters. In the
east we have Glooscap and Manabus; in the Plains
region "Old Man," who is a trickster; and in California, Coyote, who secures the sun and fire for man and
regulates all sorts of matters, but who at other times dis-
plays the stupidity and baseness of his combined animal
and human personalities.

Raven Myths. The chief mythological character on
the North Pacific Coast was Raven. The people lived
close to the shore and ravens were always about, the
most intimate and sociable of man's animal neighbors.
It is noticeable that there was an attempt to sublimate
the raven's personal characteristics by representing the
mythical hero as simply wearing a raven's robe at times
and assuming his form as a disguise. The Tlingit distinguished the hero as the Raven of the head of Nass
River, a being distinct from the common bird. There
can be no doubt, however, that the real bird has contributed much to the conception of the hero's personality and has suggested many of the grotesque incidents.
This is particularly apparent in many episodes in which
his voracious appetite is the main motive.

In the beginning according to the Haida, the sea
covered all the world, except a flat rock on which the
supernatural ones lay crisscross. Raven alighted among
these beings and then flew to the top of the sky through
which he was able to pass. Arriving in the upper

world, he displaced the chief's infant grandson. Soon after, he was dropped from his cradle and fell into the sea. A messenger invited him to a house under the water where he was given two cylindrical objects and directions for using them to make land. He bungled the matter somewhat, but the objects given him first expanded to form the Queen Charlotte Islands and then the mainland.

Among other adventures, Raven was befriended by Beavers who had a lake filled with fish and a salmon trap for catching them. Raven, taking advantage of the absence of his hosts, rolled up the lake, fish, and fishtrap and carried them away in his armpit. By this means people secured the use of fish as food. After this, Raven fell in with Eagle and, by trickery, took from him a basket of fresh water. As Eagle chased him, Raven spilled the water here and there, making the fresh water lakes and streams, also necessary that there might be fish for food. Later he got eulachon from their supernatural owner and keeper by pretending that his canoe was already smeared with eulachon grease and spawn, and distributed them at the various places where the fish are now plentiful. By changing himself into a conifer needle and floating on the drinking water he procured his birth as a child of the chief's daughter. He cried perpetually for daylight which was kept in a box by the chief until his grandfather ordered that it be given him to quiet him. Resuming his bird shape, he flew through the smoke-hole with the box and later placed the stars, moon, and sun in the sky. He secured fire by appearing among the animals at the house of the guardian of fire in the form of a deer. He tied faggots to his tail and, when the opportunity offered, set these on fire and ran out. By switching his tail against the trees he made them capable of supporting fire.

He tried to make an old woman who held the tide-line believe he had already gathered sea urchins. He blinded her and made her promise to let the tides run out twice a day instead of at much longer intervals. This made the clam digging and gathering of low-tide food possible.

At one time also he caused the waters to rise, making a flood, escaping himself by means of an arrow chain. He shot the first arrow into the sky and each succeeding one into the nock of the preceding one until he was able to climb up to the sky.

He gave the birds their various colors by painting them. His own blackness was due to his being caught in the smoke-hole of a house and being subjected to prolonged smoking.

Besides the beneficent deeds mentioned above, there were a great number of other exploits, some of which seem intended to show what might be done with unlimited magical power. There were also many in which Raven satisfied his appetite for food or sexual gratification, making use of all sorts of tricks in order to accomplish his ends.

Family Traditions. Besides those commonly known to the entire community, there were many myths and traditions connected with particular families and considered to be their private property. They were intended to account for the high standing of the family and its right to the use of houses, house furniture, certain personal names, and various ceremonial possessions. The narrative might be the bare outline of the migrations of the early ancestors. In a Kwakiutl tale, the First One, a whale, traveled in his whale canoe until he came to a desirable place, where he disembarked and built a house with certain peculiarities and having a certain name. The ancestor continued his journey, marrying the daughters of many chiefs and constantly

obtaining new names and rights which became
hereditary. The fortunes of the family were traced
down to the present and justified its claim to recognition. Another type of Kwakiutl story usually concerns
a young man of early times, who, after many purifica-
tions arrived at a house into which he is invited. The
door was alive and opened and shut; the house posts
were also alive and talked; or a woman was grown to
the floor in the house. Sometimes, as a result of marriage, but at times without, the young man was given
the house with its contents, the personal names of the
owner, and his ceremonial masks, songs, and dances.

As an example of one of these myths which explains
the history and possessions of a group, the following
abstract may be of interest. It concerns the Kwakiutl
sept, Wiwomasgem.

A Thunderbird named, Too-large, suggested to his wife that they go
down to the world beneath them. They did so and came to the mouth
of a river where a man named Only-one-on-the-beach was building a
house, unassisted. Thunderbird and his wife removed their masks,
appeared in human form, and took the names, Head-winter-dancer and
Head-winter-dance-woman. When Only-one-on-the-beach's house was
finished, he assisted the visitors in the building of their house on a hill
near a river. Here, in a short time, four sons were born to the couple.
These boys grew up with magical rapidity and were established in houses
of their own at some distance from each other. For the fourth son,
Head-winter-dancer called down his own house from the upper world
and presented it to him with a number of masks and the names and
dances belonging with them.

Head-winter-dancer had made himself a salmon weir with a trap to
hold the salmon. One morning he found in the trap a mysterious salmon
which, after some treatment, took its proper form, that of the two-headed
serpent. Just at this time a fifth son was born. When the baby was
washed, blood from the serpent was put on it and the parts so treated
turned to stone, until the boy, now twice the size of an ordinary man,
was all stone except for his neck at least, on the surface. His mother
then recognized him as the offspring of Dzonoqwa, a supernatural being

who had visited her during a fainting fit.   The boy destined to be a warrior was named Stone-body.

This man, of double stature and largely composed of stone, could not travel in an ordinary canoe.   His father then remembered that a self-propelling canoe named Paddleside-serpent-canoe had been promised him by Only-one-on-the-beach in payment for curing his sons of frogs which had infested their stomachs.   This canoe proved to be the proper means of transportation for Stone-body.   First he was taken to the houses of his four brothers and introduced to them by his father.   After that he set out to make war on the whole world, to secure slaves, wealth, names, and dances for his brothers.   The canoe transported him and his slaves at a word of command.

When he appeared near a village his shout killed or rendered insensible all the men, except the chief of the village, who immediately bought off Stone-body with slaves, skins of animals, and names with their pre-rogatives.   These, Stone-body transferred to his brothers.   Finally, Stone-body went south to Comox, a Salish settlement near Cape Mudge.   Here he secured the ceremony of the earthquake (Xwexwe). After his return, he went up a certain river, very dangerous because of its water monsters, to secure eagle down.   At a certain place, he was attacked by two brothers of his elder brother's wife, sons of one of Stone-body's victims.   They succeeded in destroying the Paddleside-serpent-canoe and in killing the crew and Stone-body himself.   They had been told he was vulnerable in his neck, the only part of his body not turned to stone.   The heads taken as trophies were carried to the village of the two brothers where they were discovered by their sister on one of her visits to her former home.   When Stone-body's relatives came for revenge, they were all killed by the two brothers who had great super-natural power.

This story, many of the details having been omitted here, explains various names of the important people in this Kwakiutl sept, why they have houses with certain carved posts and the ownership of the salmon rivers, and how they came to have the right to certain masks and dances. Several of the masks and other ceremonial objects in the Kwakiutl collection of the Museum are those mentioned in this narrative.

CHAPTER V

ART

Textile Decoration. The development of the em-
bellishment of objects of utility, in any one region is
largely dependent upon the general industries practised
there. On the Northwest Coast pottery was entirely
lacking, and clay, the material most readily modeled,
was not employed as an artistic medium. The household vessels were mostly made of wood; carving of

| Checker Design on a Mat. Kwakiutl. | Decoration produced by Varying Direction of Elements in Twilling. Kwakiutl. |

wood therefore, was the most prominent art mani-
festation. In the south, among the Salish and in the
north, among the Tlingit, basketry was well developed,
but in the main central portion of the area, except for
the hats, the baskets were crude and used for gathering
and carrying clams and similar work for which decorated
basketry was unsuitable. Mats, however, were common to the entire area. On them we find the simple,

geometric, decorative designs inherent in textile technique where the elements employed cross at right angles to each other. There were brown or black stripes; solid, or with alternating stitches of background and color. Squares and rectangles were also employed as design units. The Salish blankets and some very old examples from the northern tribes have similar decorations. Also formerly among the northern tribes

Baskets illustrating Geometrical Designs.   Tlingit.

porcupine quill embroidery quite naturally lent itself to the same sort of geometrical ornamentation.

We find, then, on the Pacific Coast, one type of art, which is common to the rest of North America. Nearly everywhere textiles were made by women, consequently, their decoration was entirely the artistic expression of women. Examples may be seen in the basketry from California and the Southwest and in the porcupine and bead embroidery of the Plains. Wherever pottery was made north of Mexico, it was also the work of the women and textile designs were often transferred to it.

On the Northwest Coast, where there was no pottery and where clothing was scanty, women's contribution to decorative art was rather limited.

Carving. The men, on the other hand, built the canoes, erected the houses, manufactured the implements employed in fishing and hunting, and provided the wooden dishes for household use. Unconstrained as it was by the limitations of the textile technique, the decorative art of the men inclined more toward realistic and grotesque representations than did that of the women. On the Northwest Coast the chief artistic expressions were through carving in the round and in relief, or through painting. The materials used for carving were wood, bone, horn, and, more recently, slate. As has been mentioned above, the Indians of this area were fortunate in the character of the available wood. The cedars are soft, straight, and fine grained and the large alders supply wood very suitable for carving with primitive implements.

The products of the women were, on the other hand, severely hampered by reason of the limitations imposed by the media. In the representative carvings and paintings of the men there was considerable opportunity for variation in form and composition, though they were naturally guided to some extent by traditional concepts of the forms portrayed. The emotions aroused in the beholders may be stirred by suggestion, through memory associations. Ordinarily, the emotional result of an artistic work is in large measure dependent upon the responses it elicits in the mind of the beholder. The better carvers of the Northwest Coast were skilful enough to portray accurately features of religious and symbolic significance. Some of the grave monuments were executed in that spirit. On the other hand, some carvings were definitely intended as realistic representa-

Haida Village of Tanu, Queen Charlotte Islands.   Photograph by
Doctor C. F. Newcombe.

Painted House Front: Thunderbird carrying off a Whale.   Alert
Bay.   Kwakiutl.

tions of animals and portraits of humans, rather than as representations of mythical monsters and personages.

Realistic art was not common on the Pacific Coast for two reasons. In a great many cases where the object carved was for a ceremonial use the animals were not realistic representations of the familiar ones of everyday life. They were either mythical beings belonging

Support of a Grave Box carved to represent a Beaver wearing a Hat. Haida.

to the supernatural past or present, or were the actual animals represented in the more nearly human form, which they were all believed to possess. In the second place, the totem poles in particular were intended to suggest a narrative, or a combination of ideas. To do this the artist took liberties with the anatomy of the animals in order to bring about the combination he desired.

Grotesque Art. It is the first motive mentioned above that was responsible for much of the grotesque nature of the art of the Northwest Coast. The Kwakiutl, for

Masks representing Supernatural Beings. Bella Coola.

example, represented a mysterious "woman" of the woods and tried to produce in her likeness the mystery and fear which the belief in her inspired. The many

masks used in the ceremonies were intended to and did
produce feelings of horror and dread especially in the
children.   The object of the ceremonies was to magnify
the power of the initiated who were believed either to be
aided by the monsters represented, or to be actually

Double Mask: Closed, Raven as a Bird; Open, Raven as a Man,
Haida.

Harpoon Rest for Bow of Canoe.   Kwakiutl.

these beings themselves.   The double-headed snake was
was one of the most powerful of the supernatural helpers
of the Kwakiutl.   Such an unnatural creature would
arouse more awe than elicited by the representation of a
snake.   In general, the Northwest Coast concept of

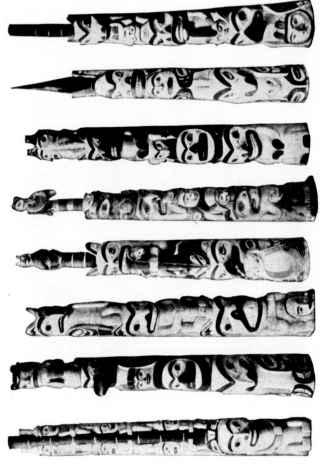

Models of Haida Totem Poles.   For Details see Swanton's *The Haida of Queen Charlotte Islands.*

supernatural power combined a considerable degree of
horror and fear. A good example is the cannibal spirit
represented as feeding on human corpses. The concept
was no less repellent to Indians than to us, and accounts
for the feeling of the supernatural at the time of the
ceremony.

Front and Back of a Box: Moon as a Bird (above) Mountain Goat
(below).

Totem Poles. Examples of connected narratives in
Northwest Coast carvings were not very numerous, but
they did occur on totem poles where some carving on the
pole served as a memory device to recall some mythological incident. More generally it was desired to

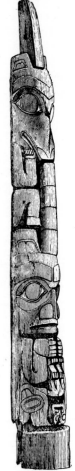

represent the main crests belonging to the family. These may have been two, three, or four, belonging to the man and his wife, and occupied prominent positions at the top, bottom, and middle of the pole. They were joined and the remaining space occupied by the representation of conventionalized animal forms, etc. It was often desired to represent animals as the ancestors of the family upon these poles and they were, therefore, shown with human faces and were distinguished from each other with difficulty.

Certain features of animals were selected as symbols and with these in mind, as keys, the figures may usually be identified. Animals were distinguished from humans by placing their ears at the top of their heads. Birds were recognized by their beaks, imposed often on an otherwise human face. Fish were indicated either by gills or fins. The three most common birds, raven, eagle, and hawk, may be distinguished by the shape of the beak: straight for the raven, curved for the eagle, and curved

Totem
Pole in the
Museum.
Haida.

Memorial
Column in the
Museum.
Haida.

until the tip rests on the mouth or chin for the hawk. Of land mammals, the beaver was represented in full by large incisor teeth, a scaly flat tail, and a stick held to his mouth with his forepaws. The grizzly bear was indicated by a large mouth full of teeth, a protruding tongue, and large paws. The killer-whale, found many times and under a great variety of conditions, was symbolized by the dorsal fin and generally also by a blow hole. Of the fishes the shark was recognized by a vaulted forehead on which are three crescents. The sculpin, in addition to gills, had two spines over its mouth.

Besides these natural animals, often shown in a human or supernatural phase, there were supernatural beings, or personified natural objects. The moon, for instance, was often shown with a circular face which resembled a hawk. The mythical thunderbird did not differ much from an eagle. If the bird were shown as bearing off a whale, the first was certainly intended. A water monster might appear in a variety of forms sometimes resembling a bear or a beaver.

It appears that heraldic and mythological art can have its full effect only when those who view it are entirely familiar with the stories and concepts which lie behind it. Since, in many cases, these myths of family origin were not fully known except to the members

Totem Pole: from below upward; Sculpin, Dogfish, Sea Monster. Haida.

Facial Paintings: Above, Beaver, Raven, Killer-whale, Dogfish; Below, Sculpin, Starfish, Mouth of Sea Monster, Proboscis of Mosquito. Haida.

150

of the family, they alone were capable of receiving the full emotional value. To some extent then the art was esoteric.

Carved Ornamentation. We may consider that the primary object of house posts, totem poles, and memorial columns was to present graphic representa-

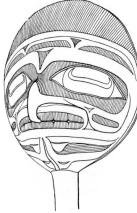

Rattle with Hawk Design.
Tlingit.

Mountain Sheep Horn Dish representing a Hawk.   Tlingit.

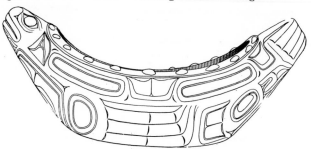

Grease Dish in Shape of a Seal.   Tlingit.

tions of varying and related concepts. If we consider other objects, such as dishes, spoons, clubs, etc., the carving becomes secondary and must supplement its use. Feast dishes possessed names and were conceived

Masks and Rattles. Woman with Labret is Represented in 2.
Haida.

as animate. They were carved in human or animal
form with a bowl in the back or belly according to the
posture chosen. Smaller oil dishes were often made to
represent a seal, in which case a fairly realistic head or
face was carved at one end and a tail at the other.
The flippers were also sometimes represented on the
two sides. The natural proportions of the animal,

Settee with Family Emblems carved on the Back.   Kwakiutl.

Paint Brushes.   Kwakiutl.

however, were subsidiary to the form imposed by the
requirements of its use as a vessel. Bowls of mountain
goat horn were given very effective representative
appearances by means of low relief carving.   Spoon
handles were somewhat more difficult because of their
tapering shape; but when once the habit of decorating
has been established, and the principle of representation
by parts has been adopted, many obstacles can be
successfully overcome.

It is generally conceded that the Northwest Coast peoples did not smoke tobacco until Europeans introduced the habit about 125 years ago. Within that time the Tlingit and Haida have carried over the carving habit from the making of spoons and rattles to pipe-making, and have produced a variety of forms.

Rearrangements and Dissections. So far, we have illustrated and discussed carving by men in the round or

Club representing a Killer-whale with Dorsal Fin bent down. Tlingit.

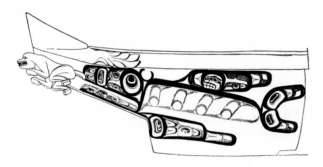

Bow of the Large Canoe in the Museum: Painting, a Killer-whale; Carving, Wolf.

in high relief. The square boxes made by folding a single straight board, as described above, also offered opportunities for decoration. These were usually carved in low relief and further embellished with color. As in the case of the dishes dug out of a single piece, it was feasible to carve the front aspect of the animal on one end, and on its rear parts the opposite end, and on the

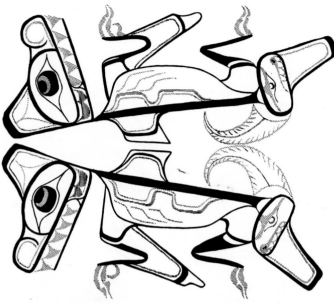

Painting a Shark cut Apart and spread Open. Haida.

Tattoo Design: a Water Monster with a
Raven's Head and a Killer-whale's Body. Haida.

Tattoo Design: Whale Monster with a Wolf's Head
shown as if Split in Two. Haida.

sides, the sides of the animal's body. Still greater
freedom was taken in this case with the relative sizes
and relations of the body parts. The liberties taken in

Painting from a House Front showing a Bear as if cut
Along the Back, giving a Symmetrical Treatment Either Side
of Circular Door.   Tsimshian.

these respects seem to have moved along these lines of
altered proportions and of an analysis of anatomical
parts amounting to actual dissection.   Frequently an

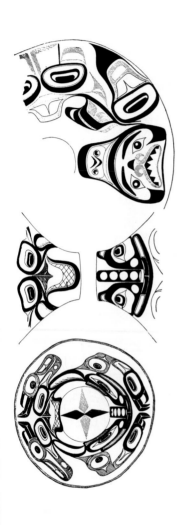

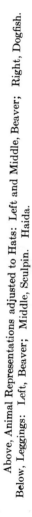

Above, Animal Representations adjusted to Hats: Left and Middle, Beaver; Right, Dogfish.
Below, Leggings: Left, Beaver; Middle, Sculpin. Haida.

157

Shirt with Designs Similar to Those on Blankets.   Tlingit.

Dancing Apron.   Tlingit.

Designs on Chilkat Blankets.

159

Designs on Chilkat Blankets.

animal was shown as if it were split from the rear to the
nose and spread out into two profiles joined in front
only.   Examples may be seen in bracelets where the
two parts of the longitudinally bisected animal encircled the wrist.   Paintings on a plane surface were also
treated in this manner, where no evident obstacle had
been the compelling cause.   In the bear split down the
back and spread open as a painted decoration on a
Tsimshian house front, it seems probable that the
bilateral natural symmetry of the animal has been

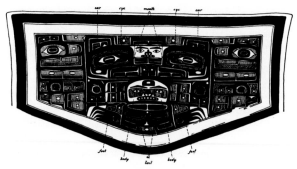

Design on Chilkat Blanket: Positions of Anatomical
Parts are Indicated.

utilized by the artist to give a symmetrical treatment
around the house entrance through the bear's navel.

Symmetry.   We have been dealing with neither realistic, nor plain symbolic art, but with a representative
art which relies for its effectiveness chiefly upon associa-
tive memory.   We discussed above the end result of a
problem of composition and symmetry.   Here the artist
employs painting and low relief carving in which the
elements of design are body parts treated with great
freedom as to their arrangement.   The composition was
adapted to the shape of the surface available for decora-

tion; the shape and relative size of body parts were adjusted to give pleasing lines. Angles gave way to curves, natural disproportions were equalized, and by the use of wider and narrower lines, or varying color, the desired results were obtained. So conventionalized had this art of dissected and freely arranged animal parts become, that the artist cut out patterns of eyes or fins and used them in drawing the outlines of his designs. Art of this sort was found on house fronts, settee backs, canoes, paddles, ends and side of boxes, skin robes, and the woven blankets of the Chilkat.

We have then on the Northwest Coast, a woman's geometric decorative art of a textile origin, similar to that found generally in North America; a man's realistic and representative art, in which the weird and mysterious are often represented; and finally, as an outgrowth of this, an elaborate conventionalized art in which body parts have been distorted from their natural anatomical form and have been given other fixed proportions according to the esthetic requirements imposed by the form of the object to be decorated.

BIBLIOGRAPHY

BOAS, FRANZ
 1890. The Houses of the Kwakiutl Indians, British Columbia (Proceedings, United States National Museum for 1888, Washington, 1890).
 1891. Sixth Report on the Northwestern Tribes of Canada (Report of the Sixteenth Meeting, British Association for the Advancement of Science, at Leeds, 1890, London, 1891).
 1895. Indianische Sagen von der Nord-Pacifischen Kuste Amerikas. Berlin, 1895.
 1897. The Social Organization and Secret Societies of the Kwakiutl Indians (Report, United States National Museum for 1895, Washington, 1897).
 1898. The Mythology of the Bella Coola Indians (Memoirs, American Museum of Natural History, vol. 2, part 2, New York, 1898).
 1921. Ethnology of the Kwakiutl (Thirty-fifth Annual Report, Bureau of American Ethnology, Washington, 1921).
 1927. Primitive Art. Instituttet for Sammenlignende Kulturforskning. Oslo, 1927.

BOAS, FRANZ, AND HUNT, GEORGE
 1902-5. Kwakiutl Texts (Memoirs, American Museum of Natural History, vol. 5, 1902–1905).
 1906. Kwakiutl Texts—Second Series (Memoirs, American Museum of Natural History, vol. 14, 1906).

COOK, CAPT. JAMES
 1785. A Voyage to the Pacific Ocean. 3 vols. Vol. 2. London, 1785.

CURTIS, EDWARD S.
 1911-1915. The North American Indians. Vols. 9, 10, 11. Cambridge, 1911–1915.

DIXON, CAPT. GEORGE
 1789. A Voyage Round the World but more Particularly to the Northwest Coast of America. London, 1789.

EMMONS, GEORGE T.
 1903. The Basketry of the Tlingit (Memoirs, American Museum of Natural History, vol. 3, part 2, 1903).
 1907. The Chilkat Blanket (Memoirs, American Museum of Natural History, vol. 3, part 4, 1907).

GUNTHER, ERNA
   1927.   Klallam Ethnography (University of Washington
             Publications in Anthropology, vol. 1, part 5,
             1927).
HAEBERLIN, HERMANN, AND GUNTHER, ERNA
   1930.   The Indians of Puget Sound (University of Washington
             Publications in Anthropology, vol. 4, part 1,
             1930).
JENNESS, DIAMOND
   1932.   The Indians of Canada (Bulletin 65, Department of
             Mines, National Museum of Canada, Ottawa,
             1932).
JEWITT, JOHN R.
   1815.   A Narrative of the Adventures and Sufferings of John
             R. Jewitt.   Middletown, 1815.
KANE, PAUL
   1859.   Wanderings of an Artist among the Indians of North
             America.   London, 1859.
KRAUSE, AUREL
   1885.   Die Tlinkit-Indianer.   Jena, 1885.
LISIANSKY, CAPT. UREY
   1814.   A Voyage Round the World in the Years 1803–1806.
             London, 1814.
MEARES, JOHN
   1790.   Voyages made in the Years 1788 and 1789 from China
             to the Northwest Coast of America.   London, 1790.
NEWCOMBE, C. F.
   1909.   Guide to Anthropological Collections in the Provincial
             Museum, Victoria, B. C.   1909.
DE LA PEROUSE, J. F. G.
   1799.   A Voyage round the World performed in the Years
             1785–1786.   2 vols. vol 1.   London, 1799.
SAPIR, EDWARD
   1922.   Sayach'apir, A Nootka Trader (In American Indian
             Life, New York, 1922).
SPROAT, G. M.
   1868.   Scenes and Studies of Savage Life.   London, 1868.
SWAN, JAMES G.
             The Indians of Cape Flattery (Smithsonian Contribu-
             tions to Knowledge, vol. 16, Washington, 1870).

SWANTON, JOHN R.
    1905a.   Haida Texts and Myths: Skidegate Dialect (Bulletin
              29, Bureau of American Ethnology, Washington,
              1905.)
    1905b.   The Haida of Queen Charlotte Islands (Memoirs,
              American Museum of Natural History, vol. 8,
              part 1, 1905).
    1905-1908. Haida Texts: Masset Dialect (Memoirs, American
              Museum of Natural History, vol. 14, part 2, 1905–
              1908).
    1908.   Social Condition, Beliefs, and Linguistic Relationship
              of the Tlingit Indians (Twenty-sixth Annual Re-
              port, Bureau of American Ethnology, Washington,
              1908).
    1909.   Tlingit Myths and Texts (Bulletin 39, Bureau of
              American Ethnology, Washington, 1909).
TEIT, JAMES
    1900.   The Thompson Indians of British Columbia (Memoirs,
              American Museum of Natural History, vol. 2,
              part 4, 1900).
    1906.   The Lillooet Indians (Memoirs, American Museum of
              Natural History, vol. 4, part 5, 1906).
    1909.   The Shuswap (Memoirs, American Museum of Natural
              History, vol. 4, part 7, 1909).
VANCOUVER, CAPT. GEORGE
    1798.   A Voyage of Discovery to the North Pacific Ocean and
              Round the World. 3 vols. London, 1798.

INDEX

Adolescence ceremonies, 97–98.
Adzes, 36, 38, 41, 43.
Alder, food dishes, 43; use of, 141.
Aleut, sea-otter hunting, 24.
Animals, conception of, 112, 113, 114; land, for food, 77–79; representation in art, 156–161; representation on totem poles, 148–149; supernatural power attributed to, 111–112.
Anklets, 80, 82.
Aprons, bark, 80, 82.
Aristocracy, concept of, 85.
Armor, types of, 106, 107.
Arrows, 76, 107.
Art, conventionalized, 162; decorative, 139–141; geometric, 162; grotesque, 144–147; Northwest Coast, 139–162; realistic, 141–143; symmetry in, 161–162.
Arts, textile, 45–58; in wood, 35–45.
Astoria, establishment of, 23–24.
Athapascan peoples, location of, 13, 14.
Ayala, don Juan de, explorations by, 21.

Bailers, for canoes, 35.
Bands, ankle, 82; woven, 48.
Bark, garments of, 82.
Basketry, 48–53, 139; Kwakiutl, 50, 51; methods of manufacture, 48–49; ornamentation of, 53, 139; techniques, 48; Tlingit, 49, 52, 53, 140.
Bathing, ritualistic, 115.
Bear, ceremony for, 116; taboos concerning, 77.
Beard, eradication of, 81.

Beaters, for bark, 54.
Beaver, in myth, 135.
Behring, explorations by, 20.
Bella Bella, first mention, 23; location of, 14; social grouping, 96; winter ceremonies, 128.
Bella Coola, beliefs about death, 133; collections from, 4; conception of supernatural, 113; deities, 112–113; divisions of year, 128; first mention, 23; inherited duties, 93; inherited honors, 92; intermarriage among, 97, 102; location of, 14; marriage regulations, 102; names and honors acquired, 92; salmon taboo, 116; social grouping, 97; winter ceremonies, 128.
Belts, cedarbark, 47.
Betrothal, potlatch for, 130.
Bird spear, 76.
Birth, supernatural control of, 112, 113.
Blankets, cedarbark, 53–55; Chilkat, 55–57, 158–161; decoration of, 140; distribution at potlatch, 131; loom for Chilkat, 55–56; Salish, 57–58, 140.
Bodega, don de la, explorations by 21.
Bone, uses of, 73, 82, 107.
Bowls, mountain goat horn, 153.
Bows, 76, 107.
Boxes, carving, 154; construction, 35, 39–41, 42, 44; decoration, 147, 154, 156, 162; uses of, 41.
Bracelets, 80, 82, 161.
Bracken roots, use as food, 74.
Brushes, used in painting, 153.

Burial, boxes used for, 41; canoe, 98; after cremation, 98–100; customs, 98–100; duties, 130; occasion for potlatch, 130; potlatch following, 130; relation of Haida social grouping to, 95–96; of relative, feast at, 88; shaman, 119, 133; tree, 98.

Camass, used for food, 75.
Cannibalism, ceremonial, 126, 127, 147.
Cannibal Society (*hamatsa*), 113, 122, 124, 126, 127.
Canoe burial, 98.
Canoes, 33–35, 109, 154; construction, 43–44; dug-out, 13; fishing in, 65; Haida, 3; for hunting porpoises, 61; important form of property, 92–93; used in transportation, 16; used in warfare, 109; whaling, 59.
Carrying straps, 48, 51.
Carved ornamentation, 151–154.
Carving, 141–146, 151–154; feast dishes, 43; tools used for, 39.
Cat's cradles, 106.
Cave burial, 98.
Cedar, uses of, 17, 19, 25, 47; used for canoes, 33; used for carvings, 141.
Cedarbark, blankets, 53–55, 82; mats, 47; uses of, 41, 46–47, 82.
Ceremonial, clothing, 81; life, 110–138; procedure in whaling, 59, 60; purity, 109, 115, 121.
Ceremonies, distribution of property at, 88; Haida, 128; master of, 122; religious, 110; Tlingit, 129; winter, 113, 119–121.
Chiefs, 86, 87, 88; rivalry of, 88–91.

Chilkat, blankets, 55–57, 159–161; houses, 31, 33; location, 13; loom, 56.
Chisels, use of, 36, 38, 40.
Clams, use as food, 73–74.
Clans, functions of, 94, 130; functions in burial, 100; system, 85, 94.
Cleanliness, ceremonial, 109, 115, 121.
Climate, Northwest Coast area, 16–17, 79.
Clothing, 79–82.
Clover, used as food, 74, 75; gardens, 75.
Clubs, for killing halibut, 65; used in seal hunting, 62; as weapons, 107, 154.
Cod, fishing for, 19, 63.
Composition, Northwest Coast art, 161–162.
Contests, Cannibal society, 127; shamanistic, 119.
Conventionalized art, 162.
Cook, Captain James, explorations of, 21.
Cooking, 73, 74, 75; utensils used in, 41.
Coppers, 89–91.
Corpse, eating by cannibal, 126, 127, 147.
Crab-apples, used for food, 74, 75.
Cradle, 82.
Creation, conception of, 134–135.
Creek-women, power of, 111.
Cremation, 98, 100.
Crests, inherited, used as tattooing designs, 83; representation on memorial columns, 100; representation on totem poles, 148.
Culture, extent of Northwest

Coast, 3, 14–15; material, 25–84.

Curing, by shaman, 117–118.

Dance pole, winter, 121.

Deadfalls, 77, 78.

Death, beliefs and customs, 132–133.

Decoration, 79–84; blanket, 140, 159–161; geometric, 53, 140, 162; on mats, 139; produced by women, 141; symmetry in, 161–162; textile, 139–141.

Deer hunting, 77.

Deformation of heads, artificial, 83, 84.

Deities, Bella Coola, 112–113; Haida, 110–112; Kwakiutl, 113–114.

Descent, counting of, Kwakiutl, 96; counting of, Haida, 95; counting of, Salish, 96; family, 13; grouping according to, 94; rules of, 85, 94–95.

Designs, 56, 139–162; animal, 157; blankets, 57, 158, 159, 160, 161; dancing apron, 158; house front, 156; tattooing, 82–83, 155.

Dice games, 106.

Digging-sticks, 73.

Discovery, Pacific Coast, 20.

Dishes, carving of, 151, 153; dug-out, 43.

Dissections, in art, 154–161.

Divination, by shamans, 118.

Divisions, exogamous, 94–96, 102.

Dixon, George, exploration by, 22.

Dog, hair, used in weaving, 57; salmon, 67.

Down, symbolic and ceremonial use, 81.

Drake, Francis, discovery of North-west Coast, 20.

Dress, 79–84; shaman's, 118–119.

Dug-out dishes, 43, 151, 153, 154.

Dyes, for basketry materials, 53; for blankets, 55; sources of, 55–56.

Eagle, adventures of, 135.

Eagles, social division, 94, 95, 112.

Ear pendants, 81.

Earrings, 82.

Earthquakes, cause of, 111; ceremony, 138.

Eel grass, use for food, 74; used in working wood, 39.

Elderberries, use for food, 74.

Emetics, use of, 115.

Engagement, marriage, 105.

Eskimo, location of, 13.

Eulachon, fishing, 68–71, 73; nets for, 46; oil, 17; oil, process of extraction, 69–70; oil, trading in, 17, 69.

Exogamous divisions, 94–96, 102.

Exploration, Northwest Coast, 20–22.

Facial painting, 150.

Family, concept of extended, 87; traditions, 136–138.

Fasting, ceremonial, 115.

Fauna, 19.

Feasts, 91–93, 94, 124, 129, 131; at mourning, 100; seal meat used for, 62; winter ceremonies, 124.

Feathers, use of, 81.

Fern roots, used for food, 74.

Fire, used in working wood, 37, 41.

Fish, baskets, 64, 67, 72; beliefs concerning, 111, 114; importance in food supply, 19, 59;

preparation for use, 63; trap, 64; weirs, 66, 67.

Fish-hooks, method of construction, 41.

Fishing, eulachon, 68–71; methods, 62–74; taboos, 116.

Floats, for hunting porpoise, 61; sealskin, used by Nootka, 35; used in whaling, 60.

Flora, 17–19.

Folklore, 133–138.

Food, accumulation for feasts, 131; dependence on sea for, 25; dishes, 43; gathering and preparation, 58–79; offerings of, 116; supply, 16, 19; taboos, 77.

Footgear, 79, 81.

Forests, 17, 19.

Forts, 106.

Framework, of houses, 25–26, 27.

Fruits, as food, 74.

Fuca, Juan de, explorations of, 20.

Fur, trade in, 22, 23–24, 81.

Future world, 132–133.

Gaff hook, 67.

Gambling, 105.

Games, 105–106.

Geometric, art, 162; decoration, 140; patterns, basketry, 53.

Girdles, 82.

Gods, Bella Coola, 112–113; Haida, 110–112; Kwakiutl, 113, 114.

Gooseberries, use for food, 74.

Grave, box, shaman's, 119; houses, 100; monuments, 132, 141, 143.

Grease trails, 17, 69.

Grotesque art, 144–147.

Groundplan, of houses, 25, 27.

Habitat, 13–19.

Haida, beliefs regarding fish, birds, and animals, 111–112; burial ceremony, 91; canoes, 34; ceremonies, 128–129; conception of origin, 134–135; cremation, 100; deities, 110–112; first description of, 22; halibut used by, 62; houses, 28, 32, 172; labret worn by woman, 82; location, 13; main potlatch, 130; marriage, 105; matrilineal groups, 102; memorial columns, 101; myths, 128; pipemaking, 154; recording of descent, 95; regard for supreme being, 110–111; shamanism, 117; social grouping, 94–95.

Hair, dress, 81; dress of shaman, 118, 121; ornament, 80.

Haisla, location of, 14.

Halibut, fishing, 19, 62–63.

Hammers, 37, 38.

Harpoons, for porpoises, 61; for salmon, 61; for seals, 61; for whaling, 59–60.

Hats, 50, 81.

Heads, artificial deformation of, 83, 84.

Heiltsuk, location of, 14.

Hemlock, 17; bark, used for food, 75.

Herring, fishing for, 73; spawn, collection of, 71.

History, early, of Northwest Coast, 20–24.

Honors, acquisition of, 86, 87, 88, 91–93, 104, 131, 132.

Hooks, for taking halibut, 62; for taking salmon, 67.

Houses, 13, 25–33; beams of, 29; Chilkat, 31–33; Haida, 28, 32; Kwakiutl, 27, 29, 31; Nootka, 27; platforms, 33; posts, 27–28;

Salish, 25–27; supernatural beings, 113, 114; Tlingit, 30.
Huckleberries, use as food, 74, 75.
Hudson Bay Company, trading by, 24.
Hunting, deer, 77; mountain goat, 77; porpoise, 61; property secured through, 93; sea-lions, 61; seals, 61–62; sea-otter, 19; whale, 59–61.

Inheritance, of clover gardens, 75; of duties, 93–94; of honors, 92; position as shaman, 117; position as chief whaling harpooner, 59; of possessions, 86, 88, 117, 137; privileges to harpoon sea-lions, 61; rights and honors, 102; rules of, 92, 96–97, 103.
Initiations, 131; into societies, 122, 124, 126.
Interior arrangement of houses, 26, 31, 32.

Jesup North Pacific Expedition, 4.

Kelp, fish, method of fishing, 63; stems, used in fishing, 62.
Killer-whale, 19, 111, 112, 113, 133, 149.
Kitlope, location of, 14.
Knives, 39, 107.
Kwakiutl, beliefs about animals, 113; blankets, 53–55; collections from, 4; conception of supernatural beings, 113–114; counting of descent, 96–97; deities, 113–114; dialects, 14; halibut fishing, 62–63; head deformation, 84; houses, 27, 29, 31; inheritance of duties, 93–94; inheritance of honors, 92; location of, 14; marriage regulations, 102, 103–105, 121, 124; names and honors acquired, 87, 88, 121; nose ornaments, 83; occasion for revenge, 107–108; oil feast, 88; porpoise hunting, 61; public accounting of property, 93; secret societies, 113, 121–127; septs, 85, 137–138; taboos, 116; a tradition of, 137–138; tree burial, 98–99; winter ceremonies, 121–127.

Labrets, 82, 152.
Lances, used in whaling, 60.
Linguistic groups, Northwest Coast, 14, 85.
Lines, for whaling harpoons, 60.
Lip plug, 82.
Lisiansky, Urey, narrative of, 24.
Loom, for cedarbark blankets, 54–55; Chilkat, 56; Salish, 58.

Mackenzie, Alexander, explorations of, 23.
Magic, performances of, 127–128.
Makah, location of, 14.
Mammals, land, as food, 19, 59, 77–79.
Marriage, customs, 85, 86, 87–88, 100–105, 124; Bella Coola, 97; honors acquired through, 87, 88, 92, 121; potlatch for, 130; regulation of, 94, 97, 102–103.
Masks, 144, 145, 152.
Master of ceremonies, function of, 122.
Material culture, Northwest Coast, 25–84.
Matrilineal groups, function of, 102.
Mats, 139–140; clothing of, 81;

method of manufacture, 46, 48, 51; use for sails, 34–35; waterproof, 81.

Maurella, don Francisco Antonio, exploration by, 21.

Meares, Captain John, explorations by, 22.

Memorial columns, 100, 101, 148.

Mending, method of, for wood, 44.

Metal, use of, 21, 81.

Moccasins, 79.

Mountain goats, hunting, 20, 77; wool, used for blanket weaving, 55, 57.

Mourning customs, 100.

Mythology, 112, 133–138.

Names, acquisition of, 91, 93, 122, 130, 131; inheritance of, 93, 96.

Nets, for crabs, 72; for eulachon fishing, 68–69; manufacture of, 45–46; for salmon, 63, 65, 67; uses, 65, 68, 69.

Nettle fiber, used in net making, 45–46.

Nootka, burial customs, 98; canoes, 35; collections from, 4; descriptions by Captain Cook, 21; houses, 92; inheritance of honors, 92; location of, 14; marriage among, 104, 105; names and honors acquired by, 91–92; negotiations, unsuccessful for transfer, 23; potlatch at maturity of girl, 98, 130; post established at, 22; puberty ceremony, 91; sea-lions hunted by, 61; sealskin floats used by, 35; taboos, 77, 116; visited by John Meares, 22; whaling among, 59–61; winter ceremonies, 121–127.

Nose, pendants, 81, 83; rings, 82.

Novice, duties of, 123, 124, 126.

Offerings, of food, 116, 133.

Oil, eulachon, preparation and use, 69; feast, form of rivalry, 88.

Ordeals, preceding marriage, 104.

Ornamentation, basketry, 53; carved, 151–154; weaving, 56, 58.

Ornaments, personal, 80, 81, 82, 83.

Pacific Coast, discovery and exploration, 20–24.

Paddles, for canoes, 34, 35.

Painting, 161.

Pattern board, Chilkat blanket, 56, 57.

Pendants, ear and nose, 82, 83.

Perez, Juan, exploration by, 20.

de la Perouse, J. T. O., explorations of, 21–22.

Pile drivers, 71.

Pipe-making, 154.

Plaiting technique, 47.

Planks, wood, method of splitting, 36, 37–38.

Platforms, in houses, 33.

Political organization, 85–109.

Porpoises, hunting of, 19, 61.

Potatoes, cultivation of, 77.

Potlatch, 129–132; burial recompensed by, 100; distribution of property at, 27; Haida, 130; meaning and social law regarding, 129–130; permanent records of, 132; at puberty, Nootka, 98; purpose, 130, 132; Tlingit, 100, 129.

Precipitation, 15, 16–17.

Property, acquisition of, 92–93; clover gardens as, 75; contests,

88–91; distribution of, 85, 88, 121, 130–131, 132; distribution at death, 100; distribution at marriage, 104; distribution at potlatch, 27, 131; importance of, Northwest Coast, 13.

Puberty, ceremonies, 97–98; feasts, 91, 130; taboos, 97.

Public accountants, duties of, 93.

Purification, for ceremonies, 109, 115, 121; preceding war, 109.

Quoits, 106.

Rainfall, 16–17, 19.

Rake, for taking herring, 73.

Rank, 85–87, 122, 132; importance of, 108; distribution of property according to, 131.

Rattle, 151, 152.

Raven, myths, 134–136.

Reeds, used for making mats, 48.

Reincarnation of animals, belief in, 111, 112, 113, 114.

Religion, 110–138.

Religious, beliefs, 110; ceremonies, 119–127; practices, 115–116.

Rivalry, of chiefs, 88–91; between groups, 127; between societies, 122; society initiations, 126; in Tlingit ceremonies, 129.

Robes, sea-otter, 81.

Roofs, construction of, 26.

Rose hips, used for food, 74.

Russians, explorations by, 24.

Sails, use on canoes, 34.

Salal berries, use for food, 74.

Salish, basketry, 139; blankets, 57–58, 140; canoe burial, 98; canoes, 33; descent and inheritance, 96; head deformation, 83; houses, 25–27; location of, 14, 15; marriage, 102, 104; mat-making, 48; salmon fishing, 63.

Salmon, berries, use as food, 74; importance in food supply, 19, 58–59; method of catching, 63–67; as people, 111, 114, 128; preparation for use, 67.

Scaffold burial, 98.

Seal, hunting of, 61–62; society, 122.

Sea-lions, hunting of, 19, 61.

Sea-otter, hunting, 19.

Seaweed, used for food, 74–75.

Secret societies, Kwakiutl, 121–127, 131.

Septs, 85, 87–88.

Settlements, Russian, 24.

Sewing, of wood, 44–45.

Shaman, burial, 119, 133; curing by, 117–118; fate of soul, 117, 133.

Shamanism, 117–119.

Shellfish, importance in food supply, 19; method of gathering, 73–74.

Shuswap, 15.

Sib system, 94.

Singers, duty of, 93.

Sinkers, use in fishing, 63.

Skidegate, 105.

Slaves, compulsory hair dress, 81; regulations regarding, 81, 86, 87, 92; securing of, cause of warfare, 107, 109.

Sleight-of-hand performances, 127, 128, 129.

Smoking, recent introduction of, 77, 154.

Social, distinctions, 85–97; grouping, 94–97; and political organization, 85–109.

Societies, secret, 119, 121–129.

Society, Seal, 122.

Songs, Kwakiutl, 93.

Soul, concept of, 132–133.

Spaniards, explorations of, 20–21.

Spawn, herring, use as food, 71, 73.

Spears, for birds, 76; salmon taken by, 63; use of, 107.

Spindles, 46, 58.

Spindle whorls, 57.

Spinning, methods of, 46, 57.

Spoons, decoration of, 153.

Spruce root, uses of, 40, 48, 49, 53.

Steam, uses in wood working, 39, 41, 44.

Stick game, 105.

Stone, tools of, 36.

Storage, household property, 26, 31.

String figures, 106.

Supernatural, beings, conception of home of, 113; beings, Bella Coola conception of, 112–113; beings, representation in art, 143, 144, 145; power, of shamans, 117; visitors, 128; world, 111.

Symbolism, carving on totem poles, 148–149.

Symmetry, in decorative art, 161–162.

Taboos, connected with whaling, 59; food, 77; hunting and fishing, 112, 114, 116; puberty, 97–98.

Tally keepers, duty of, 93.

Tattooing, 82–83; feast for, 91.

Terraces, chief's house, 33.

Textile arts, 45–58; decoration, 139–141.

Thompson Indians, 15.

Thunderbird, power of, 111, 112, 137; representation in art, 149.

Tlingit, basketry, 45, 49, 52–53, 139, 140; blanket weaving, 45; burial ceremony, 91; ceremonies, 129; cremation, 100; collections from, 4; first description of, 22; fort destroyed by, 24; houses, 30; knives, 107–108; labrets, 82; location, 13; main potlatch, 100, 130; marriage regulations, 103; matrilineal groups, 94, 102; pipe-making, 154; recording of descent, 94; shamanism, 117, 119.

Tobacco, use and cultivation, 77.

Tools, wood-working, 36–41, 54.

Topography, 15, 16.

Totem poles, 143, 146, 147–151.

Trade, in eulachon oil, 69; in fur, 23–24, 81; in grease, 17; intertribal, 14.

Trading ships, 22.

Traditions, family, 136–138.

Trails, 17.

Transportation, methods of, 16, 17, 33–34, 73, 79.

Traps, for taking animals, 78; for taking salmon, 66.

Travel, methods of, 16, 17, 33, 79, 109.

Tree, burial, 98, 99; moss, source of dye, 55.

Trees, method of felling, 36.

Tribes, Northwest Coast, 13.

Tricksters, in North American mythology, 134.

Trolling, hooks, 65; salmon taken by, 63.

Tsimshian, burial practices, 98, 100; cremation, 98; first mention of, 23; labrets, 82; location, 13–14; main potlatch, 130; marriage customs, 103; taboos, 116.

Twining technique, 48–49, 53; Chilkat blanket, 56–57.

Vancouver, Captain George, explorations of, 23.

Vegetable, fibers, clothing made from, 79; food, 59, 74–75.

Vegetation, density of, 19.

Villages, basic social units, Northwest Coast, 85; location of, 106.

Wakashan stock, dialectic groups, 14.

Walls, of houses, construction, 31.

Warclub, 108.

Warfare, 109.

Wealth, acquisition and distribution, 93; ceremonial distribution of, 86; Chilkat blankets, objects of, 57; distribution of, 91; importance of concept, 85. See Property.

Weapons, 107, 108.

Weaving techniques, 46, 47, 48; cedarbark blankets, 54; Chilkat blanket, 56–57; Salish blankets, 58.

Wedges, use in wood working. 37.

Weirs, use of, 66, 67.

Whale, tradition of, 136.

Whales, 19.

Whaling, 59–61.

Winter ceremonies, 119–129, 131.

Wolf, a social division, 94.

Wood, carving, 3, 139, 141, 143; method of bending, 39–41; method of sewing, 44; method of splitting, 37–38; used for sails, 34; work, 25, 35–45.

Wool, mountain goat, used for blankets, 55, 77, 79.

World, conception of, 110, 112, 113; future, 110, 132–133.